D0106480

SELECTED PROSE AND DRAMATIC WORK

JOHN LYLY was born in 1554. After studying at Magdalen College, Oxford and also at Cambridge, he was appointed to a position in the household of Lord Burghley. He leaped to literary prominence with the best-selling prose works of the Elizabethan period, *Euphues: The Anatomy of Wit* (1578) and *Euphues and His England* (1580). The Earl of Oxford installed him as the resident playwright at the first Blackfriars theatre, where he went on to produce a series of highly wrought comedies for performance at court. These exerted an important influence on Shakespeare. In the later 1580s the closure of the company for which he wrote brought his career to a premature halt, and he died in poverty in 1606.

LEAH SCRAGG is a senior lecturer in the Department of English and American Studies at the University of Manchester, where she has taught Renaissance drama since 1965. She has written on a range of aspects of Lylian studies. Her most recent publications include bibliographical editions of *Sapho and Phao* and *Gallathea* for the Malone Society, and a modern-spelling edition of the two parts of *Euphues* for the Revels Plays Companion Library series. She has also published a number of books and articles on Shakespeare, including *Discovering Shakespeare's Meaning*, *Shakespeare's Mouldy Tales*, and *Shakespeare's Alternative Tales*.

Fyfield*Books* aim to make available some of the great classics of British and European literature in clear, affordable formats, and to restore often neglected writers to their place in literary tradition.

Fyfield*Books* take their name from the Fyfield elm in Matthew Arnold's 'Scholar Gypsy' and 'Thyrsis'. The tree stood not far from the village where the series was originally devised in 1971.

> *Roam on! The light we sought is shining still.*
> *Dost thou ask proof? Our tree yet crowns the hill,*
> *Our Scholar travels yet the loved hill-side*

from 'Thyrsis'

JOHN LYLY

Selected Prose and Dramatic Work

Edited with an introduction by
LEAH SCRAGG

ROUTLEDGE
New York

Published in USA and Canada in 2003 by
Routledge
29 West 35th Street
New York, NY 10001
www.routledge-ny.com

Routledge is an imprint of the Taylor & Francis Group.

By arrangement with Carcanet Press Ltd.

First published in Great Britain in 1997 by Carcanet Press Ltd

This impression 2003

Selection, introduction and editorial matter Copyright © Leah
Scragg 1997, 2003

The right of Leah Scragg to be identified as the editor of this work
has been asserted by her in accordance with the Copyright, Designs
and Patents Act of 1988

All rights reserved

Cataloguing-in-Publication data is available from the Library of
Congress.
ISBN 0-415-96959-X

All rights reserved. No part of this book may be reprinted or
reproduced or utilized in any form or by any electronic, mechanical
or other means, now known or hereafter invented, including
photocopying and recording or in any information storage or
retrieval system, without permission in writing from the publishers.

Printed and bound by SRP Limited, England

Contents

Acknowledgements

The major debt of gratitude I owe in the composition of this book is undoubtedly to the Henry E. Huntington Library for the research facilities made available to me in the summer of 1991 and the spring of 1994, and to the helpfulness of the staff on both occasions. I imagine heaven may be rather like the Huntington Library. I would also like to thank the Master and Fellows of Trinity College, Cambridge, for allowing me access to their edition of *Euphues*, and the library staff for their ready assistance. I am also grateful to the Faculty of Arts Research Committee of my own university for a research support grant which enabled me to bring the later stages of this work to fruition.

Introduction

> Our nation are in his debt for a new English which he taught them. *Euphues and his England* began first that language. All our ladies were then his scholars, and that beauty in court which could not parley Euphuism was as little regarded as she which now there speaks not French.
>
> (Edward Blount (ed), *Six Court Comedies*, by John Lyly: 1632)

For twentieth-century readers looking back to the Elizabethan-Jacobean period, the figure which dominates the literary landscape is undoubtedly that of Shakespeare. For those living through the extraordinary outburst of creative activity that constitutes the English Renaissance, however, the ultimate primacy of the player from Stratford was far from self-evident. At a time when Shakespeare, newly arrived from the provinces, was still engaged in making a name for himself in the capital, Lyly was already established as the writer of the period's best-selling prose work, and as the passage quoted above (from the prefatory material to the first collected edition of his work) indicates, was credited with transforming the prose style of a generation. As the principal court dramatist of the 1580s and author of a work that had spawned a host of imitations, Lyly was for his contemporaries one of the major luminaries of the period, and it would have been difficult for them to imagine the totality of his later eclipse.

Born circa 1554,[1] Lyly was the eldest of that generation of writers known as the 'university wits'. The grandson of the grammarian, William Lily, High Master of St Paul's, he belonged to a family with strong connections with the humanist movement, and his early years followed the predictable path for one with his affiliations. Having received his education, in all probability, at the King's School, Canterbury (where Marlowe was later to be a pupil), he entered Magdalen College, Oxford, formerly attended by both his uncle and grandfather, with the apparent hope of gaining a university fellowship and embarking upon an academic career. Though he obtained his B.A. in 1573 and his M.A. in 1575, and earned himself, incidentally, a reputation as a wit, his hopes of academic preferment proved fruitless and he left Oxford for

London to advance his prospects by literary means. His success was instantaneous. His first work *Euphues: The Anatomy of Wit* (1578) was an unprecedented success, and was rapidly followed by a second, augmented, edition in 1579 and then by a sequel, *Euphues, his England*, in 1580. The prominence into which he was precipitated by the extraordinary popularity of the work (which continued to be reprinted throughout the period) attracted the notice of the Earl of Oxford through whose patronage he became a partner in the first Blackfriars theatre, embarking upon a series of plays (*Campaspe, Sappho and Phao* and *Gallathea*) designed specifically to exploit the talents of the boy actors who performed there. Though he had given no evidence of theatrical ambitions prior to his association with this troupe, Lyly clearly found the new medium a sympathetic one, and with the exception of a small number of commissioned pamphlets all his subsequent work was written for the stage. The plays produced at the Blackfriars were ultimately designed for performance at Court, his earliest dramatic ventures thus attracting the notice of Elizabeth and leading to the promise of courtly preferment. Though the Blackfriars theatre itself had ceased operation by 1584, the boys of St Paul's continued to provide Lyly with an outlet for his talents and access to the court (*Endimion, Love's Metamorphosis, Midas,* and *Mother Bombie* all belong to this period), until the suppression of this company in 1590 effectively brought his career to a close. Having dominated the literary scene for a decade he found himself overtaken by new theatrical tastes, and his single verse play, *The Woman in the Moon*, heralded as a new venture and possibly intended for the public stage, appears not to have been a success. The promise of courtly reward having yielded only the honorary position of Esquire of the Body, rather than the Mastership of the Revels as he appears at one period to have hoped, he became a Member of Parliament for a series of boroughs, but the further patronage he hoped for eluded him and he died in poverty in 1606.

The corner-stone of both Lyly's brief period of literary ascendancy, and his lasting importance in the history of the Elizabethan-Jacobean stage, is undoubtedly his development of what has become known as the euphuistic style.[2] Though the mode itself is significantly older than the prose work with which it is now associated, having roots extending into medieval Latin,[3] it was transformed by Lyly into an instrument capable of expressing a highly complex vision. At the heart of the euphuistic mode lies the use of antithetical patterning, a sentence characteristically falling into a series of paired clauses, the second matching the first syntactically but contrasting with it in meaning, with the oppositions between the two pointed by assonance and alliteration (e.g. 'Although hitherto, Euphues, I have shrined thee in my heart for a trusty friend, I will shun thee hereafter as a trothless foe', p.52). More distinctively Lylian is the insistent use of illustrative analogies drawn from classical mythology or the more fabulous aspects of natural history and which turn, like the prose style, on polarity or contradiction (e.g. 'musk, although it be sweet in the smell, is sour in the smack . . . the leaf of the cedar tree, though it be fair to be seen, yet the syrup depriveth sight', p.52). The mode clearly lends itself to (and has its origins in) debate, and familiar debate topics form the starting point for the majority of Lyly's works.

For the Elizabethan reader it would have been immediately apparent that *Euphues* is structured upon two very familiar themes. The central figure is a well-endowed young man who squanders his gifts and falls into vice, and thus corresponds to the prodigal son of the Christian parable. At the same time, the choice faced by Euphues between his friend (Philautus) and the lady (Lucilla) for whom the two men compete looks back to the love and friendship literature of the Middle Ages, a genre designed to exemplify the superiority of male comradeship to sexual love. Superficially, Lyly's work follows the expected pattern of both stories. Euphues repents of his errors like the prodigal son, and though he departs from the love and friendship tradition in sacrificing comradeship to passion, he learns from and eventually repudiates his mistake. On a deeper level, however, the meaning of the work is far more elusive than this summary of the plot suggests, and its evasiveness is primarily a product of the author's handling of the euphuistic mode.

The first phase of the work (the initial item in this selection) consists of a series of speeches linked together by a narrator, who reflects upon the issues raised by the speakers and thus orchestrates their discussion. Eubulus' first speech, for example, is followed by Euphues' lengthy riposte, and this in turn is succeeded by an address by the author who comments on the previous exchange. The encounter between Euphues and Philautus follows the same pattern. Euphues introduces himself to the young Neapolitan and proposes that they become friends, Philautus formally embraces his friendship, and the narrator comments on the bond between them. The structure clearly has its origins in the procedures of scholastic debate, but a much more complex process is at work than the straightforward articulation of, and mediation between, contrasting viewpoints. The play for voices that the author sets up develops a widening circle of oppositions that moves the reader progressively further from certainty or closure, rather than towards the rejection or endorsement of specific viewpoints.

The exchange between Eubulus and Euphues initiates the pervasive ambivalence of the work. At first sight the reader is presented with a straightforward set of oppositions. Eubulus is an old man, Euphues a young one; Eubulus advocates discipline and sobriety, Euphues the pursuit of pleasure – and in a conventional treatment of their encounter the approval of the audience would clearly lie with the more senior (and thus presumably wiser) figure. In *Euphues*, however, the development through antithetical propositions opens up a vista of alternative avenues that serves to complicate, rather than clarify, the arguments advanced. Not only is Eubulus' remonstrance countered by Euphues' retort, but the older man's own speech see-saws between oppositions, denying the reader a single perspective on the arguments advanced. Contrasting explanations are advanced, for example, to account for Euphues' wilfulness. Eubulus speculates that 'either thou didst want one to give thee good instructions, or . . . thy parents made thee a wanton with too much cockering, either they were too foolish in using no discipline or thou too froward in rejecting their doctrine' (p.6). The series of paired clauses here serves to present the reader with alternative versions of the hero's infancy, and thus of the reasons for his present condition. Was he a neglected child, or a pampered one? Does the fault lie in his own disposition, or with his parents? The question is left open, while the path to amendment becomes equally problematic. The acquisition of virtue, Eubulus argues, may be achieved through the observation of vice (p.7), inviting the reader to speculate whether the existence of vice is essential to the apprehension of virtue, while he suggests that those who aspire the highest are in the greatest danger of falling, and hence calls in question the worth of pursuing perfection (p.8). The uncertainties generated by these observations (of which only a few have been touched on here) are heightened by Euphues' riposte. The core of Eubulus' argument is that it is the duty of the parent to train the child, and he advances a series of illustrations, largely drawn from the natural world, in order to justify his point:

> Did they [Euphues' parents] not remember that which no man ought to forget, that the tender youth of a child is like the tempering of new wax, apt to receive any form? He . . . that coveteth to have a straight tree must not bow him being a twig. The potter fashioneth his clay when it is soft, and the sparrow is taught to come when he is young. As, therefore, the iron being hot receiveth any form with the stroke of the hammer, and keepeth it being cold for ever, so the tender wit of a child, if with diligence it be instructed in youth, will with industry use those qualities in his age. (p.6)

Euphues, naturally, rejects this proposition, and he too uses the natural world in order to support his position:

> You bewray your own weakness in thinking that nature may anyways be altered by education; and as you have ensamples to confirm your pretence, so I have most evident and infallible arguments to serve for my purpose. It is natural for the vine to spread: the more you seek by art to alter it, the more in the end you shall augment it. It is proper for the palm-tree to mount: the heavier you load it the higher it sprouteth. Though iron be made soft with fire it returneth to his hardness; though the falcon be reclaimed to the fist she retireth to her haggardness. (p.10)

Here, not only do these propositions counter those previously advanced, but the illustrations themselves open up a paradoxical universe in which actions breed their contraries and a process of transmutation is constantly at work. Pruning a vine merely encourages its growth, while loading down a palm tree causes its height to increase. Hard substances may become malleable and then hard again, while wild creatures may be made tractable, but will once more grow wild.

A comparable set of opposing positions is set up by Lucilla when she contemplates renouncing her love of Philautus in favour of Euphues. Concerned that her new lover will doubt her capacity for faithfulness in view of the fact that she has changed her affections, she argues:

> Ah fond wench, dost thou think Euphues will deem thee constant to him, when thou hast been unconstant to his friend? Weenest thou that he will have no mistrust of thy faithfulness, when he hath had trial of thy fickleness? . . . Well doth he know that the glass once crazed will with the least clap be cracked, that the cloth which staineth with milk will soon lose his colour with vinegar . . . that she that hath been faithless to one will never be faithful to any. (p.25)

The examples appear to offer a convincing justification for the view that one lapse will lead inevitably to a greater, but the speaker then proceeds to turn her own argument on its head, supporting the opposite position with an equally convincing set of illustrations:

> But can Euphues convince me of fleeting, seeing for his sake I break my fidelity? . . . May he justly condemn me of treachery, who hath this testimony as trial of my good will? Doth not he remember that the broken bone once set together is stronger than ever it was; that the greatest blot is taken off with the pumice; that though the spider poison the fly, she cannot infect the bee; that although I have been light to Philautus, yet I may be lovely to Euphues? (p.25-6)

Weakness now is seen not as a prelude to further failure but an index of future strength, faithlessness leads to fidelity, while the stained cloth becomes capable of metamorphosis into a stainless fabric.

The dual potentialities of the natural world, implicit in the illustrations that the speakers employ, are reiterated in the imagery of the work as a whole. The reader is informed that love is 'not unlike the fig-tree, whose fruit is sweet, [but] whose root is more bitter than the claw of a bittern', or 'like the apple in Persia, whose blossom savoureth like honey, [but] whose bud is more sour than gall' (p.28); that 'in painted pots is hidden the deadliest poison . . . in the greenest grass is the greatest serpent, in the clearest water the ugliest toad' (p.21). Just as each clause and each sentence is made up of antithetical elements, so too is the physical universe, and ultimately the conceptual realm. Moreover, the characters of the story conform in both their doubleness of nature and capacity for change to the universe in which they exist. Euphues himself corresponds to the painted pot of poison in his behaviour towards Philautus, making an outward show of friendship while planning to destroy his happiness, while he undergoes a metamorphosis from a faithful friend into a faithless one, and back into a faithful friend again. Lucilla appears to be the clearest water to Philautus in disdaining his friend Euphues, but plays the part of the ugliest toad in secretly encouraging his rival's passion, while she loves and then hates Philautus, desires and rejects Euphues, and ultimately gives herself to Curio whom she knows, paradoxically, to be worthless. Similarly, Philautus embraces Euphues, repudiates, and re-accepts him, while Ferardo is proud and then ashamed of his daughter. In short, where the taut symmetrical construction of euphuistic prose with its illustrative analogies suggests the precise, quasi-scientific, enunciation and exploration of ideas, it in fact sets up for the reader a constantly mutating world, in which there is nothing, to quote the narrator, 'but that hath his contraries' (p.15). It is this evasiveness which is the hallmark of Lyly's later compositions and which makes him, in the words of his first editor, such a 'witty companion'.

Campaspe (1583), the first of Lyly's plays for the first Blackfriars theatre, while seeming at first sight to constitute a radical departure for the writer of the period's most celebrated prose work, might in fact be described with some justice as Euphues transferred to the stage. Though the narrator has given place to a Prologue, and the speeches of which the previous composition largely

consisted now succeed one another without authorial interven-
tion, the euphuistic mode is employed throughout, while the
world projected remains one of contrasting states and ambivalent
natural phenomena. Once again the work is based upon a number of conventional debate motifs, including the proper conduct
of a monarch, the rights and duties of the subject, and the relative
value of the martial and intellectual pursuits. The first lines of Act
I, for example, spoken by Clitus, one of Alexander's followers, set
up the characteristic dialectical structure, with oppositions pointed
by alliteration, and the location of ambiguity in both the physical
and intellectual spheres:

> Parmenio, I cannot tell whether I should more commend in
> Alexander's victories courage or courtesy, in the one being a
> resolution without fear, in the other a liberality above custom:
> Thebes is razed, the people not racked; towers thrown down,
> bodies not thrust aside; a conquest without conflict, and a
> cruel war in a mild peace. (I.i.1-6)

While seeming at first glance to be simply an elegantly phrased
tribute to an exceptionally merciful victor, these lines prove on
closer inspection to be far richer in implication. They invite the
audience to consider which of the two aspects of Alexander's
conduct (courage or courtesy) is the more commendable, and
thus initiate the first of the play's debate motifs, while they simul-
taneously evoke a world engaged in a process of change ('Thebes
is razed': 'towers thrown down'), in which similarity may mask
difference ('a conquest without conflict') and contraries co-exist
('a cruel war in a mild peace'). As in *Euphues*, moreover, the alternatives propounded within this opening speech are then expanded into wider oppositions between speakers. Just as the opinions
of Eubulus and Euphues are juxtaposed in the prose work, so the
views of Timoclea and her conquerors are set against one another
when the captive Thebans are introduced:

> *Parmenio.* Madam, you need not doubt; it is Alexander that is
> the conqueror.
> *Timoclea.* Alexander hath overcome, not conquered.

Parmenio. To bring all under his subjection is to conquer.
Timoclea. He cannot subdue that which is divine.
Parmenio. Thebes was not.
Timoclea. Virtue is.   (I.i.49-55)

Here, the see-saw motion of the syntax is now enacted between speakers, while the exchange destabilizes the meaning of the terms that the two parties employ. As Timoclea points out, if 'to conquer' means 'to bring all under his subjection' as Parmenio maintains, then Alexander has not conquered the Thebans, as he has not subdued their moral will, further complicating the assessment of the play's central figure initiated in the opening lines.

A further extension of the antithetical patterning pervasive in the work takes place through the contrastive relationship set up by the dramatist between scenes. Act I scene i begins with balanced oppositions within a single speech and moves to a species of debate, but it concludes with a statement of intention that appears to invite the approbation of the audience and thus to function as a species of certainty. Alexander announces his determination to marry his skills as a soldier to the knowledge of a philosopher, and thus to become an ideal ruler, and this seemingly unexceptionable proposition is met with considerable enthusiasm by his principal officer, Hephestion:

Your Majesty therein showeth that you have as great desire to rule as to subdue, and needs must that commonwealth be fortunate whose captain is a philosopher, and whose philosopher is a captain.   (I.i.101-4)

This statement, which concludes the scene, is followed by the entrance of three boys, two of whom serve philosophers and one of whom is starving. Their exchanges immediately call Hephestion's judgement into question, revealing Diogenes' incapacity to govern the petty commonwealth of the household. The relationship between the two scenes extends the ambivalences surrounding the nature of kingship initiated in earlier exchanges, and this process is continued through the shifting stances of the dramatis personae themselves. Alexander, for example, having fallen in love

xv

with Campaspe, declares 'Alexander doth love and therefore must obtain . . . I am a king and will command' (II.ii.110-15), only to counter this view of his potency on resigning her to Apelles with the observation that a king 'cannot subdue the affections of men, though he conquer their countries' (V.iv.143-4). Similarly, Hephestion declares in I.iii that if he were Alexander he would 'leave war to study wisdom' (116), but finds himself increasingly regretting the 'rust' that has 'crept into [his] bones' (V.iv.6) as a consequence of the protracted peace.

Just as the antithetical organization of euphuistic prose feeds into the structuring of speech and scene, and into the characters' oscillation between opposing positions, so Lyly's distinctive imagery finds its way from the printed page to the theatrical event. As in *Euphues*, the field of reference in *Campaspe* evokes an unstable world compounded of contrasting properties, with arguments supported by illustrations turning on the ambivalent nature of natural phenomena. The audience is informed, for example, that 'Basil softly touched yieldeth a sweet scent, but chafed in the hand a rank savour' (Prologue at the Blackfriars, 14-16), that the 'mugil, of all fishes the swiftest, is found in the belly of the bret, of all the slowest' (II.ii.60-1), that 'ermines have fair skins but foul livers, sepulchres fresh colours but rotten bones' (II.ii.65-6). The insistent ambiguity generated by these illustrations is supported, moreover, by word play, most notably the use of homophones (e.g. 'O Thebes, thy walls were raised by the sweetness of the harp, but razed by the shrillness of the trumpet': I.i.38-9) and punning (e.g. the play on 'cry' in III.ii). A widening circle of ambiguity is thus established that moves outwards from the single word to the balanced sentence, from the sentence to contrasting scenes and ultimately to the entire structure of the play. Whereas the action appears to move to a firm conclusion, with Alexander conquering his affections, renouncing Campaspe to his rival Apelles, and leading his troops once again into war, the terms through which this process is accomplished work against the sense of closure, implying that the king's affections have waned rather than that he has conquered his passion, and that he has failed to find a fit role for himself as monarch in times of peace:

xvi

Go, Apelles, take with you your Campaspe. Alexander is cloyed
with looking on that which thou wonderedst at. (V.iv.155-7)

Let the trumpet sound, strike up the drum, and I will presently
into Persia . . . And good Hephestion, when all the world is
won and every country is thine and mine, either find me out
another to subdue or, of my word, I will fall in love. (V.iv.163-
75)

The concluding lines of the drama thus create a sense of circular-
ity rather than of linear development, leaving the audience
poised at the close between opposing ways of viewing the play's
progress.

Whereas in *Euphues* the evasiveness with which the author
treats his inherited motifs is implicit in the organization of the
work, in *Campaspe* the play's elusiveness is an explicit aspect of
authorial design. The audience is informed by the Prologue at the
Court that 'Whatsoever we present, we wish it may be thought
the dancing of Agrippa his shadows, who, in the moment they
were seen, were of any shape one would conceive' (13-16), while
the Epilogue at the Blackfriars defines the drama as fluid and
unstable, its final meaning determined not by the dramatist but
by the spectator; cf., 'Our exercises must be as your judgement is,
resembling water, which is always of the same colour into what it
runneth' (5-7). The second of Lyly's plays for the first Blackfriars
(*Sappho and Phao*, 1583) reiterates the multiplicity of meaning to
which the dramatist aspires, presenting the audience with a
'labyrinth of conceits' (Epilogue, line 3)[4] but it was *Gallathea*, the
third item in this collection, which constituted Lyly's supreme
achievement during this period in the structured representation
of an unstable world. Once again, the audience is presented with
a dramatic idiom rich in antithetical constructions, iterative
image patterns insistently exhibiting the inherent doubleness of
natural phenomena, and a series of variations upon conventional
debate motifs (e.g. love versus chastity). In this play, however,
every aspect of the dramatic structure contributes to the presen-
tation of a world engaged in a constant process of change, in
which everything has the potential to become its opposite and
may be viewed, therefore, in contrasting ways.

The entrance of an old man and a youth at the start of the play initiates both the antithetical balancing and insistent ambivalence that are characteristic of the drama as a whole. The visual opposition between the two speakers is complicated by the fact that the younger is immediately addressed as 'Gallathea', creating uncertainty over his/her sexual identity. This epicene figure then enquires the causes of her altered form, and is supplied with an explanation that involves the audience in a series of changing perceptions of the location in which the action takes place:

> In times past, where thou seest a heap of small pebble, stood a stately temple of white marble, which was dedicated to the god of the sea . . . Hither came all such as either ventured by long travel to see countries, or by great traffic to use merchandise, offering sacrifice by fire to get safety by water, yielding thanks for perils past, and making prayers for good success to come. But Fortune, constant in nothing but inconstancy, did change her copy as the people their custom, for the land being oppressed by Danes, who instead of sacrifice committed sacrilege, instead of religion, rebellion, and made a prey of that in which they should have made their prayers, tearing down the temple even with the earth, being almost equal with the skies, enraged so the god who binds the winds in the hollows of the earth that he caused the seas to break their bounds, sith men had broke their vows, and to swell as far above their reach as men had swerved beyond their reason. Then might you see ships sail where sheep fed, anchors cast where ploughs go, fishermen throw their nets where husbandmen sow their corn, and fishes throw their scales where fowls do breed their quills. (I.i.15-36)

Here, not only is there the characteristic seesaw between antithetical elements ('offering sacrifice by fire to get safety by water'), with oppositions pointed through sound patterning, specifically the use of homophones and alliteration ('made a prey of that in which they should have made their prayers'), but the story the speaker unfolds involves a series of transmutations. The scene in which the action is set was once a place of piety, and then of impiety, and is now the site (as we gather in his following speech) of a sacrificial rite. A much-frequented temple was reduced to a 'heap of small pebble', while the land became sea, and then land again, and, as we subsequently learn, is once more threatened with inundation. This movement between antithetical states and the doubleness of perception to which it gives rise is then extended to every aspect of the ensuing drama. Characters disguise themselves as their opposites, the two aspects of their composite personalities exhibiting themselves in different contexts. Gallathea and Phillida, for instance, both disguised as boys, are youths to one another and to Diana's nymphs who fall in love with them, while remaining girls in the eyes of their fathers. The scenes in which these changes of role are initiated, moreover, function as antithetical versions or mirror images of one another. Gallathea's imposed disguise as a boy, for example, is reversed in Cupid's voluntary role as a nymph, while Phillida's assumption of a masculine form in order to evade a god's revenge is mirrored in Cupid's maiden guise designed to enact one. These outward changes, in turn, form the prelude to other species of transformation. Diana's nymphs, committed to chastity, fall in love with the seeming youths, while Neptune, bent on destruction, finally works for reconciliation. Roles are reversed, too, in other senses. Mortal men (e.g. the Alchemist and Astronomer) seek to usurp the role of the gods, while Cupid declines from a 'great god' (I.ii.34) to Diana's 'slave' (V.iii.36). At the same time, the emotions experienced by the characters also prove to be compounded of opposites (love, for example, is 'a heat full of coldness, a sweet full of bitterness, a pain full of pleasantness': I.ii.18-19), while the dramatis personae are subject to an immutable destiny which proves to be changeable and a fortune that is 'constant in nothing but inconstancy' (I.i.22-3).

The ambivalence that invades every aspect of the play world gives rise to a similar instability of audience response. Hebe, for example, led unjustly to the sacrifice, engages sympathy as she laments the violent death that awaits her:

> Miserable and accursed Hebe, that being neither fair nor fortunate, thou shouldst be thought most happy and beautiful.

Curse thy birth, thy life, thy death, being born to live in danger, and, having lived, to die by deceit . . . The Egyptians never cut their dates from the tree, because they are so fresh and green; it is thought wickedness to pull roses from the stalks in the garden of Palestine, for that they have so lively a red . . . Shall it only be lawful amongst us in the prime of youth and pride of beauty to destroy both youth and beauty, and what was honoured in fruits and flowers as a virtue, to violate in a virgin as a vice?   (V.ii.8-25)

The monster does not appear, however, to claim the sacrifice, and Hebe, after a brief moment of joy at her release from danger immediately plunges into another lament:

Fortunate Hebe, how shalt thou express thy joys? Nay, unhappy girl, that art not the fairest. Had it not been better for thee to have died with fame than to live with dishonour, to have preferred the safety of thy country and rareness of thy beauty before sweetness of life and vanity of the world? . . . I would, Hebe, thou hadst been beautifullest.   (V.ii.67-74)

Here, not only does the character's view of the situation undergo an abrupt change, but so does that of the theatre audience. An occasion of sorrow is now perceived as a cause for joy, and an occasion of joy as a cause for sorrow. Death is now seen as preferable to life, and escape from defloration as a source of shame. Similar shifts of perception attend other strands of the drama (e.g. the dispute between Cupid and the nymphs of Diana) with the audience poised between conflicting responses to the situations that the playwright presents. As Cupid ruefully remarks in relation to his own plight, it remains uncertain whether even the most partisan of spectators will seek to 'revenge it for despite or laugh at it for disport' (IV.ii.74-5).

Though the use of the euphuistic mode confirms the affinity between Lyly's prose and dramatic works, the corpus of plays represented by the two comedies in this collection were undoubtedly written to be performed rather than read. The talents of the boy actors are exploited throughout, with opportunities for singing, dancing and tumbling (as in *Campaspe*, V.i.1-49), while scenes of agile word play rather than profound emotion confirm the dramatist's awareness of the strengths and limitations of his troupe. Youths figure among the dramatis personae of both plays (the servants of *Campaspe* and the apprentices of *Gallathea*), while the epicene character of pre-pubescent boys is exploited in the many female roles (e.g. the nymphs of Diana) and the sexual ambivalences of *Gallathea*. At the same time, stage spectacle contributes to the projection of meaning. In *Campaspe*, for example, the tub of the philosopher Diogenes and the workshop of the painter Apelles provide the audience with a visual opposition corresponding to the antithetical balancing at work in other aspects of the drama. Diogenes' tub represents a life of privation, while Apelles' workshop constitutes an arena in which the life of the senses is celebrated. By bringing his martial hero to either location the dramatist sets up a further set of oppositions – between a life of action rather than reflection when he moves to Diogenes' tub, and of arms versus arts when he visits the workshop. Similarly, the oak-tree, which in the opening scene of *Gallathea* offers welcome shade to Tyterus and his daughter, functions as a constant reminder to the audience of the threat hanging over the dramatis personae when it is revealed to be the site of the virgin sacrifice. Meaning is communicated, moreover, through action, rather than arising solely from speech. The entrance of Diana's nymphs with the captive Cupid in *Gallathea* IV.ii, for example, signals the triumph of chastity over love, while the unpicking of love knots in the same scene is emblematic of the reversal that has taken place in Cupid's state.

As the Prologues and Epilogues to the two plays indicate, however, it was not solely questions of staging that Lyly had in mind when his plays were composed. The comedies written for the first Blackfriars were conceived with a view to performance at Court, and are designed to appeal to a specific audience. *Campaspe* is concerned with issues of major importance to Elizabeth herself – the relationship between the public and private selves of the monarch, the responsibilities of the sovereign, and the nature and extent of a ruler's power – while *Gallathea* may be seen as contributing to the cult of the virgin Queen in its celebration of the triumph of Diana (frequently associated with Elizabeth) over Cupid. The highly polished style, word play and insistent classical references proclaim the intellectual character of the drama, while the audience is flattered by the inference that such sophisticated compositions must seem crude by the standards of the court (see *Campaspe*, The Prologue at the Court, 1-2). Nevertheless, it would be a mistake to assume that these comedies may be dismissed as wholly sycophantic. Though superficially deferential, they deftly resist (as noted above) yielding up a single 'meaning', their ambivalences admitting a rather more sceptical interrogation of ideological issues than is frequently assumed. While Alexander's encounter with Campaspe, for example, explores the proper role of the monarch, it also considers the rights (and exposes the vulnerability) of the subject, while the fulsome opening speeches on Alexander's virtues are countered by darker views on the realities of political power (I.iii.74-89 and IV.iii.26-9). Similarly, *Gallathea*, does not move towards the unequivocal celebration of Diana and her nymphs. Their treatment of Cupid, although justifiable on one level, evokes sympathy on another, while it is the potency of love rather than the virtue of chastity that is affirmed in the closing lines. Above all the emphasis upon change, and upon the inherent ambivalence of all human experience, works against the overt celebration of an immutable, peerless authority – inviting the audience to delight with the dramatist in the endless possibilities of an unstable world.

As a result of the rapidity of Lyly's eclipse following the emergence of a new generation of Elizabethan dramatists, his first editor was obliged, in 1632, not merely to remind his readers of his author's former prominence (see the opening lines of this Introduction) but to justify the publication of his work. The twentieth-century editor, faced with a similar situation some three hundred and fifty years later, can do no better than echo his words:

A sin it were to suffer these rare monuments of wit to lie covered in dust, and a shame such conceited comedies should be acted by none but worms . . . These his plays crowned him with applause and the spectators with pleasure. Thou canst not repent the reading of them over. When . . . John Lyly is

xxii

merry with thee in thy chamber, thou shalt say few, or none, of our poets now are such witty companions – and thank me that brings him to thy acquaintance.

Leah Scragg

Notes

1. For further biographical information see Albert Feuillerat, *John Lyly: Contribution à l'Histoire de la Renaissance en Angleterre*, Cambridge University Press, 1910; G.K. Hunter, *John Lyly: The Humanist as Courtier*, London, 1962; and Mark Eccles, *Brief Lives: Tudor and Stuart Authors* (*Studies in Philology*, Texts and Studies), 1982, to all of which I am indebted here.

2. The following discussion of the relationship between Lyly's prose and dramatic work is based upon my '*Any Shape One Would Conceive*: From a Prose Style to Lyly's plays for the First Blackfriars Theatre', a paper delivered at a symposium on 'Contexts of Comedy', University of Trømso, 1993, to be published in *Contexts of Renaissance Comedy*, ed. Janet Clare and Roy Eriksen (Oslo, 1997). The discussion of the use of spectacle was first presented as part of a paper delivered at a conference on 'Writing and Ideas *c.*1590', University of York, 1995.

3. For a detailed account of the evolution of the euphuistic mode, see Morris William Croll and Harry Clemons (eds), *Euphues the Anatomy of Wit: Euphues His England*, London, 1916, pp. xv-lxiv.

4. Quoted from G.K. Hunter and David Bevington (eds), *Campaspe: Sappho and Phao*, Manchester University Press, 1991.

Note on the Texts

The three works in this collection are all drawn from the first phase of Lyly's career, from his arrival in London to the closure of the first Blackfriars theatre (with which *Gallathea*, the last item, is thought to have been associated). All three have been edited from the earliest editions, *Euphues* (1578) (of which only the narrative portion is represented here) from the copy in the library of Trinity College, Cambridge, and *Campaspe* (pub. 1584) and *Gallathea* (pub. 1592) from the quartos in the Huntington Library. Readings have been checked against all major modern editions (see Select Bibliography below) and in the case of *Euphues* against James Winny's old spelling, *The Descent of 'Euphues'* (Cambridge University Press, 1957), and of *Campaspe* against the text in A.K. McIlwraith (ed.) *Five Elizabethan Comedies* (Oxford University Press, 1934). All these editions have contributed in some way to the decisions made in the course of the present work and it is impossible to record my overall debt to each. Specific points of dependence, however, are acknowledged in the notes.

Since this edition is designed for the student or general reader, the text has been modernized throughout, while proper names have been regularized and appear in their modern forms. The process of modernization, while rendering the texts accessible to a twentieth-century reader, obscures in some instances the word play which is a characteristic feature of Lyly's work, and the original readings are recorded in the notes where multiple meanings would otherwise be lost. In the case of the plays, editorial additions to the stage directions are indicated by square brackets, as are the very few corrections to the largely excellent copy texts. The songs performed by the boy actors of Lyly's plays are not preserved in the quartos, but a number were recovered by Edward Blount for his *Six Court Comedies* (1632), the first collected edition of Lyly's dramatic work. The two editions of the *Court Comedies* in the Huntington Library have been collated for the present work, and the songs (enclosed in square brackets) appear as in Blount's text. Some of the songs, however, have clearly been lost, and their absence is signalled in the notes.

The passage from *Euphues* constitutes the only modern spelling edition of the original 1578 text without the later additions.

Select Bibliography

The standard edition of Lyly's dramatic and non-dramatic works remains R. Warwick Bond's old-spelling *The Complete Works of John Lyly*, 3 vols, Oxford, 1902 (reprinted 1967 and 1973), the cornerstone of twentieth-century Lylian scholarship. Of almost equal importance for students of *Euphues* is Morris William Croll and Harry Clemons (eds), *Euphues the Anatomy of Wit: Euphues His England*, London, 1916 (reprinted 1964), a fully annotated, modern-spelling edition of the two parts of Lyly's major prose work, with a substantial introduction on the history of the euphuistic mode. Of the relatively few critical editions that have appeared in recent years, Carter A. Daniel, *The Plays of John Lyly*, London and Toronto, 1988, offers a lightly annotated, modern spelling edition of the entire dramatic corpus, while Anne B. Lancashire, *Gallathea and Midas*, Regents Renaissance Drama Series, University of Nebraska, 1969, and G.K. Hunter and David Bevington, *Campaspe: Sappho and Phao*, Revels Plays, Manchester University Press, 1991, are more richly annotated and include substantial introductions. A modern-spelling edition of the narrative portion of *Euphues* in its augmented (1579) form may be found in Paul Salzman, *An Anthology of Elizabethan Prose Fiction*, Worlds Classics, Oxford University Press, 1987, which includes selections from other sixteenth-century prose works and a helpful bibliography.

While the scholarly impetus in the first half of the twentieth century was largely editorial and biographical (see Albert Feuillerat's monumental *John Lyly: Contribution à l'Histoire de la Renaissance en Angleterre*, Cambridge University Press, 1910), the period subsequent to the Second World War has seen a substantial reassessment of Lyly's achievement. G.K. Hunter's pioneering *John Lyly: The Humanist as Courtier*, London, 1962, locates both *Euphues* and the comedies within the context of the humanist movement, while Jonas A. Barish, 'The Prose Style of John Lyly', *English Literary History* 23 (1956), pp. 14-35 demonstrates the relationship between style and vision in Lyly's work. Outstanding among studies devoted exclusively to the plays is Peter Saccio, *The Court Comedies of John Lyly*, Princeton University Press, 1969, which highlights the pervasive ambivalence of the universe that the dramatist projects, a theme also pursued in *The Metamorphosis of 'Gallathea': a Study in Creative Adaptation*,

Washington D.C., 1982, my own investigation of the influence of *Gallathea* on the Shakespearian corpus.

For those embarking on the study of John Lyly, Joseph W. Houppert, *John Lyly*, Twayne's English Authors Series, Boston, 1975, includes a useful survey of the history of Lylian criticism, while my 'John Lyly' in *Dictionary of Literary Biography*, vol. 62, ed. Fredson Bowers, Detroit, 1987, pp. 196-211 offers a brief critical introduction to both the dramatic and non-dramatic work. The most recent study of the plays is Michael Pincombe, *The Plays of John Lyly: Eros and Eliza*, in the Revels Plays Companion Library series, Manchester University Press, 1996.

EUPHUES
THE ANATOMY OF WIT

There dwelt in Athens a young gentleman of great patrimony and of so comely a personage that it was doubted whether he were more bound to Nature for the lineaments of his person or to Fortune for the increase of his possessions. But Nature, impatient of comparisons, and as it were disdaining a companion or copartner in her working, added to this comeliness of his body such a sharp capacity of mind that not only she proved Fortune counterfeit but was half of that opinion that she herself was only current.[1] This young gallant, of more wit than wealth, and yet of more wealth than wisdom, seeing himself inferior to none in pleasant conceits, thought himself superior to all in honest conditions, insomuch that he deemed himself so apt to all things that he gave himself almost to nothing but practising of those things commonly which are incident to these sharp wits – fine phrases, smooth quipping, merry taunting, using jesting without mean, and abusing mirth without measure. As therefore the sweetest rose hath his prickle, the finest velvet his brack,[2] the fairest flour his bran, so the sharpest wit hath his wanton will, and the holiest head his wicked way. And true it is that some men write, and most men believe, that in all perfect shapes a blemish bringeth rather a liking every way to the eyes than a loathing any way to the mind. Venus had her mole in her cheek which made her more amiable; Helen her scar on her chin which Paris called *cos amoris*, the whetstone of love;[3] Aristippus his wart,[4] Lycurgus his wen.[5] So likewise in the disposition of the mind, either virtue is over-

[1] *counterfeit . . . current*] metaphor drawn from coining, signifying Fortune to be without true influence and Nature alone of worth   [2] *brack*] flaw
[3] *Helen . . . love*] legendary beauty, wife of Menelaus, whose abduction by Paris, son of King Priam, was the cause of the Trojan War   [4] *Aristippus*] Greek philosopher (*c*.435-366 BC), disciple of Socrates and founder of the hedonistic school   [5] *Lycurgus . . . wen*] Athenian orator (*c*.390-*c*.324 BC), noted for his integrity. His 'wen' (i.e. growth) appears to be ahistorical.

shadowed with some vice or vice overcast with some virtue: Alexander[6] valiant in war, yet given to wine; Tully[7] eloquent in his glozes,[8] yet vainglorious; Solomon wise, yet too too wanton; David holy, but yet an homicide;[9] none more witty than Euphues, yet at the first none more wicked.

The freshest colours soonest fade, the teenest[10] razor soonest turneth his edge, the finest cloth is soonest eaten with moths, and the cambric[11] sooner stained than the coarse canvas. Which appeared well in this Euphues, whose wit being like wax apt to receive any impression, and having the bridle in his own hands either to use the rein or the spur, disdaining counsel, leaving his country, loathing his old acquaintance, thought either by wit to obtain some conquest, or by shame to abide some conflict, and leaving the rule of reason, rashly ran unto destruction.

It hath been an old said saw,[12] and not of less truth than antiquity, that wit is the better if it be the dearer bought; as in the sequel of this history shall most manifestly appear. It happened this young imp[13] to arrive at Naples (a place of more pleasure than profit, and yet of more profit than piety), the very walls and windows whereof showed it rather to be the tabernacle of Venus than the temple of Vesta.[14] There was all things necessary and in readiness that might either allure the mind to lust, or entice the heart to folly: a court more meet for an atheist than for one of Athens, for Ovid than for Aristotle,[15] for a graceless lover than for a godly liver; more fitter for Paris than Hector,[16] and meeter

---

[6]   *Alexander*] conqueror, and founder of the Macedonian monarchy (b.356 BC)
[7]   *Tully*] Marcus Tullius Cicero, Roman orator (106-43 BC)   [8]   *glozes*] expositions   [9]   *Solomon . . . homicide*] Biblical patriarchs, the former noted for his wisdom but also for the thousand wives and concubines who turned his heart away from God, the latter beloved of God but guilty of the death of Uriah
[10]   *teenest*] sharpest   [11]   *cambric*] fine white linen fabric   [12]   *saw*] wise saying or maxim   [13]   *imp*] person of noble lineage   [14]   *tabernacle of Venus . . . temple of Vesta*] a place dedicated to love (Venus) rather than chastity (Vesta, goddess of the hearth, attended by virgins)   [15]   *Ovid / Aristotle*] celebrated Roman poet (43 BC-17 AD) noted for his *Ars Amatoria (Art of Love)* / Greek philosopher (384-322 BC), profoundly interested in ethics   [16]   *Paris / Hector*] sons of Priam, King of Troy. Paris the seducer of Helen (see above note 3) / Hector the heroic defender of the city

4

for Flora than Diana.[17] Here my youth (whether for weariness he could not or for wantonness would not go any further) determined to make his abode; whereby it is evidently seen that the fleetest fish swalloweth the delicatest bait, that the highest soaring hawk traineth to the lure, and that the wittiest sconce[18] is inveigled with the sudden view of alluring vanities.

Here he wanted no companions, which courted him continually with sundry kinds of devices, whereby they might either soak his purse to reap commodity, or soothe his person to win credit, for he had guests and companions of all sorts. There frequented to his lodging and mansion house as well the spider to suck poison of his fine wit as the bee to gather honey, as well the drone as the dove, the fox as the lamb, as well Damocles to betray him as Damon[19] to be true to him. Yet he behaved himself so warily that he could single out his game wisely[20] insomuch that an old gentleman in Naples, seeing his pregnant wit, his eloquent tongue somewhat taunting yet with delight, his mirth without measure yet not without wit, his sayings vainglorious yet pithy, began to bewail his nurture and to muse at his nature, being incensed against the one as most pernicious and inflamed with the other as most precious. For he well knew that so rare a wit would in time either breed an intolerable trouble, or bring an incomparable treasure to the common weal; at the one he greatly pitied, at the other he rejoiced. Having, therefore, gotten opportunity to communicate with him his mind, with watery eyes, as one lamenting his wantonness, and smiling face, as one loving his wittiness, encountered him on this manner:

'Young gentleman, although my acquaintance be small to entreat you, and my authority less to command you, yet my good will in giving you good counsel should induce you to believe me, and my hoary hairs (ambassadors of experience) enforce you to follow me; for by how much the more I am a stranger to you, by so much the more you are beholding to me. Having, therefore,

---

[17] *Flora / Diana*] goddesses of the spring and chastity, the former associated with licentiousness through the nature of the celebration of her festival
[18] *sconce*] head   [19] *Damocles / Damon*] archetypes of flattery and faithful friendship   [20] *single . . . wisely*] selected shrewdly among the herd

opportunity to utter my mind, I mean to be importunate with you to follow my meaning. As thy birth doth show the express and lively image of gentle blood, so thy bringing up seemeth to me to be a great blot to the lineage of so noble a brute;[21] so that I am enforced to think that either thou didst want one to give thee good instructions, or that thy parents made thee a wanton with too much cockering,[22] either they were too foolish in using no discipline or thou too froward in rejecting their doctrine, either they willing to have thee idle or thou wilful to be ill employed. Did they not remember that which no man ought to forget, that the tender youth of a child is like the tempering of new wax, apt to receive any form? He that will carry a bull with Milo must use to carry him a calf also,[23] he that coveteth to have a straight tree must not bow him being a twig. The potter fashioneth his clay when it is soft, and the sparrow is taught to come when he is young.[24] As, therefore, the iron being hot receiveth any form with the stroke of the hammer, and keepeth it being cold for ever, so the tender wit of a child, if with diligence it be instructed in youth, will with industry use those qualities in his age.

'They might also have taken example of the wise husband-men,[25] who in their fattest[26] and most fertile ground sow hemp before wheat, a grain that drieth up the superfluous moisture, and maketh the soil more apt for corn; or of good gardeners, who in their curious knots[27] mix hyssop with thyme as aiders the one to the growth of the other, the one being dry, the other moist; or of cunning painters, who for the whitest work cast the blackest ground, [28] to make the picture more amiable. If, therefore, thy father had been as wise an husbandman as he was a fortunate husband, or thy mother as good a housewife as she was a happy wife, if they had been both as good gardeners to keep their knot as they were grafters to bring forth such fruit, or as cunning painters as

---

[21] *brute*] offspring of a heroic line   [22] *cockering*] pampering
[23] *bull . . . also*] A reference to the Greek athlete, Milo (6th century BC), famous for feats of strength, including carrying a bull on his shoulders through the stadium at Olympia.   [24] *sparrow . . . young*] sparrows were frequently kept as pets in the sixteenth century   [25] *husbandmen*] farmers
[26] *fattest*] heaviest, i.e. most sticky with moisture   [27] *curious knots*] intricately patterned formal gardens   [28] *ground*] background

they were happy parents, no doubt they had sowed hemp before wheat, that is discipline before affection, they had set hyssop with thyme, that is manners with wit, the one to aid the other; and to make thy dexterity more, they had cast a black ground for their white work, that is they had mixed threats with fair looks.

'But things past are past calling again, it is too late to shut the stable door when the steed is stolen. The Trojans repented too late when their town was spoiled. Yet the remembrance of thy former follies might breed in thee a remorse of conscience, and be a remedy against further concupiscence. But now to thy present time. The Lacedaemonians[29] were wont to show their children drunken men and other wicked men, that by seeing their filth they might shun the like fault, and avoid such vices when they were at the like state. The Persians to make their youth abhor gluttony would paint an Epicure[30] sleeping with meat in his mouth and most horribly overladen with wine, that by the view of such monstrous sights they might eschew the means of the like excess. The Parthians, to cause their youth to loathe the alluring trains[31] of women's wiles and deceitful enticements, had most curiously carved in their houses a young man blind, besides whom was adjoined a woman so exquisite, that in some men's judgement Pygmalion's image[32] was not half so excellent, having one hand in his pocket as noting their theft, and holding a knife in the other hand to cut his throat.

'If the sight of such ugly shapes caused a loathing of the like sins, then, my good Euphues, consider their plight, and beware of thine own peril. Thou art here in Naples a young sojourner, I an old senior, thou a stranger, I a citizen, thou secure doubting no mishap, I sorrowful dreading thy misfortune. Here mayest thou see that which I sigh to see, drunken sots wallowing in every house, in every chamber, yea, in every channel;[33] here mayest thou behold that which I cannot without blushing behold, nor without blubbering utter, those whose bellies be their gods, who

---

[29] *Lacedaemonians*] Spartans, noted for their austere lifestyle [30] *Epicure*] follower of Epicurus (341-270 BC), who taught that pleasure is the highest good [31] *trains*] trail designed to lure or entrap [32] *Pygmalion's image*] statue of a woman so beautiful that the sculptor (Pygmalion) fell in love with it. The tale occurs in Ovid's *Metamorphoses*. [33] *channel*] gutter

7

offer their goods as sacrifice to their guts, who sleep with meat in their mouths, with sin in their hearts, and with shame in their houses. Here, yea here, Euphues, mayest thou see, not the carved vizard[34] of a lewd woman, but the incarnate visage of a lascivious wanton, not the shadow of love, but the substance of lust. My heart melteth in drops of blood to see a harlot with the one hand rob so many coffers, and with the other to rip so many corpses. Thou art here amidst the pikes,[35] between Scylla and Charybdis,[36] ready if thou shun Syrtis to sink into Symplegades.[37] Let the Lacedaemonian, the Persian, the Parthian, yea, the Neapolitan cause thee rather to detest such villainy at the sight and view of their vanity.

'Is it not far better to abhor sins by the remembrance of others' faults than by repentance of thine own follies? Is not he accounted most wise whom other men's harms do make most wary? But thou wilt haply say that although there be many things in Naples to be justly condemned, yet there are some things of necessity to be commended, and as thy will doth lean unto the one, so thy wit would also embrace the other.

'Alas, Euphues, by how much the more I love the high climbing of thy capacity, by so much the more I fear thy fall. The fine crystal is sooner crazed than the hard marble, the greenest beech burneth faster than the driest oak, the fairest silk is soonest soiled, and the sweetest wine turneth to the sharpest vinegar. The pestilence doth most rifest[38] infect the clearest complexion, and the caterpillar cleaveth unto the ripest fruit; the most delicate wit is allured with small enticement unto vice, and most subject to yield unto vanity. If, therefore, thou do but hearken to the Sirens[39] thou wilt be enamoured, if thou haunt their houses and places thou shalt be enchanted.

---

[34] *vizard*] mask   [35] *pikes*] pointed rocks (i.e. equally dangerous alternatives   [36] *Scylla and Charybdis*] dangerous rock and whirlpool lying between Italy and Sicily   [37] *Syrtis and Symplegades*] sand bar and group of floating islands said to lie in the Euxine Sea   [38] *rifest*] readily   [39] *Sirens*] mythological birds with the faces of virgins, who lured mariners to land with the sweetness of their voices and killed them

'One drop of poison infecteth the whole tun of wine, one leaf of Coloquintida[40] marreth and spoileth the whole pot of porridge, one iron-mole defaceth the whole piece of lawn.[41] Descend into thine own conscience and consider with thyself the great difference between staring and stark-blind, wit and wisdom, love and lust. Be merry but with modesty, be sober but not too sullen, be valiant but not too venturous. Let thy attire be comely but not costly, thy diet wholesome but not excessive, use pastime as the word importeth – to pass the time in honest recreation. Mistrust no man without cause, neither be thou credulous without proof. Be not light to follow every man's opinion, nor obstinate to stand in thine own conceit. Serve God, love God, fear God, and God will so bless thee as either heart can wish or thy friends desire. And so I end my counsel, beseeching thee to begin to follow it.'

This old gentleman having finished his discourse, Euphues began to shape him an answer in this sort: 'Father and friend (your age showeth the one, your honesty the other), I am neither so suspicious to mistrust your good will, nor so sottish to mislike your good counsel; as I am therefore to thank you for the first, so it stands upon me to think better on the latter. I mean not to cavil with you as one loving sophistry, neither to control you as one having superiority; the one would bring my talk into the suspicion of fraud, the other convince[42] me of folly.

'Whereas you argue, I know not upon what probabilities but sure I am upon no proof, that my bringing-up should be a blemish to my birth, I answer, and swear too, that you were not therein a little overshot; either you gave too much credit to the report of others, or too much liberty to your own judgement. You convince my parents of peevishness in making me a wanton, and me of lewdness in rejecting correction. But so many men so many minds; that may seem in your eye odious which in another's eye may be gracious. Aristippus a philosopher, yet who more courtly?

---

[40] *Coloquintida*] bitter apple (a purgative)   [41] *iron-mole / lawn*] blemish cause by iron rust / fine linen   [42] *convince*] convict

Diogenes a philosopher, yet who more carterly?[43] Who more popular than Plato, retaining always good company? Who more envious than Timon, denouncing all human society? Who so severe as the Stoics, which like stocks[44] were were moved with no melody? Who so secure as the Epicures which wallowed in all kind of licentiousness? Though all men be made of one metal, yet they be not cast all in one mould. There is framed of the self-same clay as well the tile to keep out water as the pot to contain liquor, the sun doth harden the dirt and melt the wax, fire maketh the gold to shine and the straw to smother, perfumes doth refresh the dove and kill the beetle, and the nature of the man disposeth that consent of the manners.[45]

'Now whereas you seem to love my nature and loathe my nurture, you bewray your own weakness in thinking that nature may anyways be altered by education; and as you have ensamples to confirm your pretence,[46] so I have most evident and infallible arguments to serve for my purpose. It is natural for the vine to spread: the more you seek by art to alter it, the more in the end you shall augment it. It is proper for the palm-tree to mount: the heavier you load it the higher it sprouteth. Though iron be made soft with fire it returneth to his hardness; though the falcon be reclaimed to the fist she retireth to her haggardness;[47] the whelp of a mastiff will never be taught to retrieve the partridge; education can have no show where the excellency of nature doth bear sway. The silly mouse will by no manner of means be tamed; the subtle fox may well be beaten, but never broken from stealing his prey; if you pound spices they smell the sweeter; season the wood never so well, the wine will taste of the cask; plant and translate the crab-tree where and whensoever it please you and it will never bear sweet apple. Infinite and innumerable were the

[43] *carterly*] boorish. The references in this and the following sentences are to schools of philosophy. For Aristippus see above, n. 4; Diogenes, principal cynic philosopher (died *c.* 320 BC); Plato, originator of the doctrine of *ideas* (*c.* 428-347 BC); Timon, a sceptic (*c.* 320-*c.*230 BC). The Stoics believed that the virtuous mind was impregnable to misfortune. For the Epicures see above, n. 30.
[44] *stocks*] tree stumps   [45] *nature . . . manners*] the character of the individual determines his behaviour.   [46] *pretence*] position
[47] *haggardness*] wild state

examples I could allege and declare to confirm the force of nature and confute these your vain and false forgeries, were not the repetition of them needless, having showed sufficient, or bootless, seeing those alleged will not persuade you. And can you be so unnatural, whom Dame Nature hath nourished and brought up so many years, to repine as it were against Nature?

'The similitude you rehearse of the wax argueth your waxing and melting brain, and your example of the hot and hard iron showeth in you but cold and weak disposition. Do you not know that which all men do affirm and know, that black will take no other colour; that the stone Asbeston being once made hot will never be made cold; that fire cannot be forced downward; that Nature will have course after kind;[48] that everything will dispose itself according to Nature? Can the Ethiop change or alter his skin, or the leopard his hue? Is it possible to gather grapes of thorns, or figs of thistles, or to cause anything to strive against Nature?

'But why go I about to praise Nature, the which as yet was never any imp so wicked and barbarous, any Turk so vile and brutish, any beast so dull and senseless, that could, or would, or durst dispraise or contemn? Doth not Cicero conclude and allow that if we follow and obey Nature we shall never err? Doth not Aristotle allege and confirm that Nature frameth or maketh nothing in any point rude, vain, and unperfect? Nature was had in such estimation and admiration among the heathen people that she was reputed for the only goddess in heaven. If Nature, then, have largely and bountifully endued me with her gifts, why deem you me so untoward[49] and graceless? If she have dealt hardly[50] with me, why extol you so much my birth? If Nature bear no sway, why use you this adulation? If Nature work the effect, what booteth any education? If Nature be of strength or force, what availeth discipline or nurture? If of none, what helpeth Nature? But let these sayings pass as known evidently and granted to be true, which none can, or may, deny unless he be false, or that he be an enemy to humanity.

---

[48] *have course after kind*] follow its natural bent   [49] *untoward*] refractory, backward   [50] *hardly*] meanly

11

'As touching my residence and abiding here in Naples, my youthly and lusty affections, my sports and pleasures, my pastimes, my common dalliance, my delights, my resort and company, and companions which daily use to visit me, although to you they breed more sorrow and care than solace and comfort because of your crabbed age, yet to me they bring more comfort and joy than care and grief, more bliss than bale, more happiness than heaviness, because of my youthful gentleness. Either you would have all men old as you are, or else you have quite forgotten that you yourself were young or ever know young days; either in your youth you were a very vicious and ungodly man, or now being aged very superstitious and devout above measure.

'Put you no difference between the young flourishing bay-tree and the old withered beech? No kind of distinction between the waxing and the waning of the moon, and between the rising and the setting of the sun? Do you measure the hot assaults of youth by the cold skirmishes of age, whose years are subject to more infirmities than our youth? We merry, you melancholy; we zealous in affection, you jealous[51] in all your doings; you testy without cause, we hasty for no quarrel; you careful, we careless; we bold, you fearful; we in all points contrary unto you, and ye in all points unlike unto us.

'Seeing therefore we be repugnant each to the other in nature, would you have us alike in qualities? Would you have one potion ministered to the burning fever and to the cold palsy; one plaster to an old issue[52] and a fresh wound; one salve for all sores; one sauce for all meats? No, no, Eubulus! But I will yield to more than either I am bound to grant, either thou able to prove. Suppose that which I never will believe, that Naples is a cankered storehouse of all strife, a common stews[53] for all strumpets, the sink of shame, and the very nurse of all sin: shall it therefore follow of necessity that all that are wooed of love should be wedded to lust; will you conclude, as it were *ex consequenti*, that whosoever arriveth here shall be enticed to folly and being enticed of force shall be entangled? No, no, it is the disposition of the thought that altereth the nature of the thing. The sun shineth upon the dunghill

---

[51] *jealous*] suspicious   [52] *issue*] discharge of blood   [53] ' *stews*] brothel

12

and is not corrupted, the diamond lieth in the fire and is not consumed, the crystal toucheth the toad and is not poisoned, the bird trochilus liveth by the mouth of the crocodile and is not spoiled,[54] a perfect wit is never bewitched with lewdness neither enticed with lasciviousness.

'Is it not common that the holm-tree springeth amidst the beech; that the ivy spreadeth upon the hard stones; that the soft feather-bed breaketh the hard blade? If experience have not taught you this, you have lived long and learned little, or if your moist brain have forgot it, you have learned much and profited nothing. But it may be that you measure my affections by your own fancies, and knowing yourself either too simple to raise the siege of policy, or too weak to resist the assault by prowess, you deem me of as little wit as yourself, or of less force; either of small capacity, or of no courage. In my judgement, Eubulus, you shall as soon catch a hare with a tabor[55] as you shall persuade youth with your aged and overworn eloquence to such severity of life, which as yet there was never Stoic so strict, nor Jesuit so superstitious, neither votary so devout, but would rather allow it in words than follow it in works, rather talk of it than try it. Neither were you such a saint in your youth that, abandoning all pleasures, all pastimes, and delights, you would choose rather to sacrifice the first fruits of your life to vain holiness than to youthly affections. But as to the stomach quatted[56] with dainties all delicates seem queasy, and as he that surfeiteth with wine useth afterward to allay with water, so these old huddles,[57] having overcharged their gorges with fancy, account all honest recreation mere folly, and having taken a surfeit of delight, seem now to savour it with despite.

'Seeing therefore it is labour lost for me to persuade you and wind vainly wasted for you to exhort me, here I found you and here I leave you, having neither bought nor sold with you but changed ware for ware. If you have taken little pleasure in my

---

[54] *liveth . . . spoiled*] supports itself from the [pickings in the] crocodile's mouth and is not destroyed   [55] *catch a hare with a tabour*] proverbial, signifying an impossible task. The maxim may refer to the animal's acute hearing (cf. 'It is ill catching hares with drums').   [56] *quatted*] glutted   [57] *huddles*] disrespectful term for the aged

reply, sure I am that by your counsel I have reaped less profit. They that use to steal honey burn hemlock to smoke the bees from their hives; and it may be that to get some advantage of me you have used these smoky arguments, thinking thereby to smother me with the conceit of strong imagination. But as the chameleon though he have most guts draweth least breath, or as the elder tree though he be fullest of pith is farthest from strength, so though your reasons seem inwardly to yourself somewhat substantial, and your persuasions pithy in your own conceit, yet being well weighed without, they be shadows without substance and weak without force. The bird taurus hath a great voice but a small body;[58] the thunder a great clap yet but a little stone; the empty vessel giveth a greater sound than the full barrel. I mean not to apply it, but look into yourself and you shall certainly find it; and thus I leave you seeking it, but were it not that my company stay my coming I would surely help you to look it, but I am called hence by my acquaintance.'

Euphues, having thus ended his talk, departed, leaving this old gentleman in a great quandary; who, perceiving that he was more inclined to wantonness than to wisdom, with a deep sigh, the tears trickling down his cheeks, said: 'Seeing thou wilt not buy counsel at the first hand good cheap, thou shalt buy repentance at the second hand at such an unreasonable rate that thou wilt curse thy hard pennyworth and ban[59] thy hard heart.' And immediately he went to his own house, heavily bewailing the young man's unhappiness.

Here ye may behold, gentlemen, how lewdly wit standeth in his own light, how he deemeth no penny good silver but his own,[60] preferring the blossom before the fruit, the bud before the flower, the green blade before the ripe ear of corn, his own wit before all men's wisdoms. Neither is that geason,[61] seeing for the most part it is proper to all those of sharp capacity to esteem of themselves as most proper. If one be hard in conceiving they pronounce him a dolt, if given to study they proclaim him a dunce;

[58] *The bird taurus*] mythological creature, ultimately derived from Pliny's *Historia Naturalis*   [59] *ban*] utter execrations upon   [60] *no penny . . . own*] no coin current except his own (i.e. no ideas valid except his own)   [61] *geason*] out of the ordinary

14

if merry a jester, if sad a saint; if full of words a sot, if without speech a cipher; if one argue with them boldly then is he impudent, if coldly an innocent; if there be reasoning of divinity they cry *Quae supra nos nihil ad nos*, if of humanity *Sententias loquitur carnifex*.[62] Hereof cometh such great familiarity between the ripest wits when they shall see the disposition the one of the other, the *sympathia* of affections, and as it were but a pair of shears to go between their natures.[63] One flattereth an other in his own folly, and layeth cushions under the elbow of his fellow[64] when he seeth him take a nap with fancy; and as their wit wresteth them to vice, so it forgeth them some feat[65] excuse to cloak their vanity.

Too much study doth intoxicate their brains. 'For,' say they, 'although iron the more it is used the brighter it is, yet silver with much wearing doth waste to nothing; though the cammock[66] the more it is bowed the better it serveth, yet the bow the more it is bent and occupied[67] the weaker it waxeth; though the camomile the more it is trodden and pressed down the more it spreadeth, yet the violet the oftener it is handled and touched the sooner it withereth and decayeth. Besides this, a fine wit, a sharp sense, a quick understanding, is able to attain to more in a moment or a very little space than a dull and blockish head in a month. The scythe cutteth far better and smoother than the saw, the wax yieldeth better and sooner to the seal than the steel to the stamp or hammer, the smooth and plain beech is easier to be carved and occupied than the knotty box. For neither is there anything but that hath his contraries.'

Such is the nature of these novices that think to have learning without labour, and treasure without travail; either not understanding, or else not remembering, that the finest edge is made with the blunt whetstone, and the fairest jewel fashioned with the hard hammer. I go not about, gentlemen, to inveigh against wit,

---

[62] *Quae supra nos nihil ad nos / Sententias loquitur carnifex*] that which is above us is nothing to us / The executioner pronounces sentence (i.e. there can be no disinterested judgement in the matter).   [63] *pair . . . natures*] proverbial. Cut out of the same material (i.e. of the same disposition)   [64] *layeth . . . fellow*] panders to his companion (i.e. encourages him in his folly)
[65] *feat*] deft   [66] *cammock*] crook   [67] *occupied*] used

for then I were witless, but frankly to confess mine own little wit. I have ever thought so superstitiously of wit that I fear I have committed idolatry against wisdom; and if Nature had dealt so beneficially with me to have given me any wit, I should have been readier in the defence of it to have made an apology, than any way to turn to apostasy. But this I note, that for the most part they stand so on their pantofles[68] that they be secure of perils, obstinate in their own opinions, impatient of labour, apt to conceive wrong, credulous to believe the worst, ready to shake off their old acquaintance without cause, and to condemn them without colour. All which humours are by so much the more easier to be purged, by how much the less they have festered the sinews. But return we again to Euphues.

Euphues having sojourned by the space of two months in Naples, whether he were moved by the courtesy of a young gentleman named Philautus or enforced by destiny, whether his pregnant wit or his pleasant conceits wrought the greater liking in the mind of Euphues, I know not for certainty, but Euphues showed such entire love towards him that he seemed to make small account of any others, determining to enter into such an inviolable league of friendship with him as neither time by piecemeal should impair, neither fancy utterly dissolve, nor any suspicion infringe. 'I have read,' saith he, 'and well I believe it, that a friend is in prosperity a pleasure, a solace in adversity, in grief a comfort, in joy a merry companion, at all times another I, in all places the express image of mine own person, insomuch that I cannot tell whether the immortal gods have bestowed any gift upon mortal men either more noble or more necessary than friendship. Is there anything in the world to be reputed (I will not say compared) to friendship? Can any treasure in this transitory pilgrimage be of more value than a friend, in whose bosom thou mayest sleep secure without fear, whom thou mayest make partner of all thy secrets without suspicion of fraud, and partaker of all thy misfortune without mistrust of fleeting,[69] who will account thy bale his bane,[70] thy mishap his misery, the pricking of thy

---

[68] *stand . . . pantofles*] literally, stand so much on their high-heeled shoes (i.e. their dignity)   [69] *fleeting*] fickleness   [70] *thy bale his bane*] your woe his ruin

finger the piercing of his heart? But whither am I carried? Have I not also learned that one should eat a bushel of salt with him whom he meaneth to make his friend? That trial maketh trust? That there is falsehood in fellowship? And what then? Doth not the sympathy of manners make the conjunction of minds? Is it not a byword,[71] like will to like? Not so common as commendable it is to see young gentlemen choose them such friends with whom they may seem, being absent to be present, being asunder to be conversant,[72] being dead to be alive. I will therefore have Philautus for my fere,[73] and by so much the more I make myself sure to have Philautus, by how much the more I view in him the lively image of Euphues.'

Although there be none so ignorant that doth not know, neither any so impudent that will not confess friendship to be the jewel of human joy, yet whosoever shall see this amity grounded upon a little affection will soon conjecture that it shall be dissolved upon a light occasion; as in the sequel of Euphues and Philautus you shall see, whose hot love waxed soon cold. For as the best wine doth make the sharpest vinegar, so the deepest love turneth to the deadliest hate. Who deserved the most blame in mine opinion it is doubtful, and so difficult that I dare not presume to give verdict. For love being the cause for which so many mischiefs have been attempted, I am not yet persuaded whether of them was most to be blamed, but certainly neither of them was blameless. I appeal to your judgement, gentlemen, not that I think any of you of the like disposition able to decide the question, but, being of deeper discretion than I am, are more fit to debate the quarrel. Though the discourse of their friendship and falling out be somewhat long, yet, being somewhat strange, I hope the delightfulness of the one will attenuate the tediousness of the other.

Euphues had continual access to the place of Philautus and no little familiarity with him, and finding him at convenient leisure, in these short terms unfolded his mind unto him.

'Gentleman and friend, the trial I have had of thy manners

---

[71] *byword*] proverbial saying   [72] *asunder . . . conversant*] apart . . . in constant association   [73] *fere*] comrade

cutteth off divers terms which to another I would have used in the like matter. And sithence a long discourse argueth folly, and delicate words incur the suspicion of flattery, I am determined to use neither of them, knowing either of them to breed offence. Weighing with myself the force of friendship by the effects, I studied ever since my first coming to Naples to enter league with such a one as might direct my steps, being a stranger, and resemble my manners, being a scholar; the which two qualities as I find in you able to satisfy my desire, so I hope I shall find a heart in you willing to accomplish my request. Which, if I may obtain, assure yourself that Damon to his Pythias, Pylades to his Orestes, Titus to his Gysippus, Theseus to his Pyrothus, Scipio to his Laelius,[74] was never found more faithful than Euphues will be to his Philautus.'

Philautus by how much the less he looked for this discourse, by so much the more he liked it, for he saw all qualities both of body and mind in Euphues; unto whom he replied as followeth:

'Friend Euphues (for so your talk warranteth me to term you), I dare neither use a long process, neither loving speech, lest unwittingly I should cause you to convince me of those things which you have already condemned. And verily I am bold to presume upon your courtesy, since you yourself have used so little curiosity, persuading myself that my short answer will work as great an effect in you as your few words did in me. And seeing we resemble (as you say) each other in qualities, it cannot be that the one should differ from the other in courtesy; seeing the sincere affection of the mind cannot be expressed by the mouth and that no art can unfold the entire love of the heart, I am earnestly to beseech you not to measure the firmness of my faith by the fewness of my words, but rather think that the overflowing waves of goodwill leave no passage for many words. Trial shall prove trust. Here is my hand, my heart, my lands, and my life at thy commandment. Thou mayest well perceive that I did believe thee, that so soon I did love thee; and I hope thou wilt the rather love me, in that I did believe thee.'

After many embracings and protestations one to another, they

[74] *Damon . . . Laelius*] all common examples of exemplary friendship

18

walked to dinner, where they wanted neither meat,[75] neither music, neither any other pastime; and having banqueted, to digest their sweet confections, they danced all that afternoon. They used not only one board,[76] but one bed, one book (if so be it they thought not one too many). Their friendship augmented every day, insomuch that the one could not refrain the company of the other one minute. All things went in common between them, which all men accounted commendable.

Philautus being a town-born child, both for his own continuance and the great countenance[77] which his father had while he lived, crept into credit with Don Ferardo, one of the chief governors of the city, who, although he had a courtly crew of gentlewomen sojourning in his palace, yet his daughter, heir to his whole revenues, stained the beauty of them all, whose modest bashfulness caused the other to look wan for envy, whose lily cheeks dyed with a vermilion red made the rest to blush at her beauty. For as the finest ruby staineth the colour of the rest that be in place, or as the sun dimmeth the moon that she cannot be discerned, so this gallant girl, more fair than fortunate, and yet more fortunate than faithful, eclipsed the beauty of them all and changed their colours. Unto her had Philautus access, who won her by right of love and should have worn her by right of law, had not Euphues by strange destiny broken the bonds of marriage and forbidden the banns of matrimony.

It happened that Don Ferardo had occasion to go to Venice about certain his own affairs, leaving his daughter the only steward of his household, who spared not to feast Philautus her friend with all kinds of delights and delicates, reserving only her honesty[78] as the chief stay of her honour. Her father being gone, she sent for her friend to supper, who came not, as he was accustomed, solitarily alone but accompanied with his friend, Euphues. The gentlewoman, whether it were for niceness or for niggardness of courtesy,[79] gave him such a cold welcome that he repented that he was come.

---

[75] *meat*] food   [76] *board*] dining table   [77] *continuance / countenance*] persistence / reputation   [78] *honesty*] chastity   [79] *for niceness or for niggardness of courtesy*] through over-refinement or want of manners

Euphues, though he knew himself worthy every way to have a good countenance,[80] yet could he not perceive her willing any way to lend him a friendly look. At the last, supper being ready to come in, Philautus said unto her: 'Gentlewoman, I was the bolder to bring my shadow with me' (meaning Euphues), 'knowing that he should be the better welcome for my sake.' Unto whom the gentlewoman replied: 'Sir, as I never when I saw you thought that you came without your shadow, so now I cannot a little marvel to see you so overshot[81] in bringing a new shadow with you.'

Euphues, though he perceived her coy nip,[82] seemed not to care for it, but taking her by the hand said: 'Fair lady, seeing the shade doth often shield your beauty from the parching sun, I hope you will the better esteem of the shadow; and by so much the less it ought to be offensive by how much the less it is able to offend you, and by so much the more you ought to like it by how much the more you use to lie in it.'

'Well, gentleman,' answered Lucilla, 'in arguing of the shadow we forgo the substance. Pleaseth it you, therefore, to sit down to supper?' And so they all sat down; but Euphues fed of one dish which ever stood before him, the beauty of Lucilla. Here Euphues at the first sight was so kindled with desire that almost he was like to burn to coals.

Supper being ended, the order was in Naples that the gentlewomen would desire to hear some discourse, either concerning love or learning. And although Philautus was requested, yet he posted it over to Euphues, whom he knew most fit for that purpose. Euphues, being thus tied to the stake[83] by their importunate entreaty, began as followeth:

'He that worst may is alway enforced to hold the candle; the weakest must still to the wall; where none will, the devil himself must bear the cross.[84] But were it not, gentlewomen, that your

---

[80] *countenance*] reception   [81] *overshot*] excessive   [82] *coy nip*] disdainful jibe   [83] *tied to the stake*] forced into compliance. The metaphor is drawn from bear-baiting.   [84] *He that worst . . . cross*] all proverbial. *To hold the candle to one's shames*: to expose one's own failings. *The weakest goeth to the wall*: the feeblest are always exposed or obliged to give place. *Where none may the devil must bear the cross*: the least able are sometimes obliged to perform a task.

list[85] stands for law, I would borrow so much leave as to resign mine office to one of you, whose experience in love hath made you learned, and whose learning hath made you so lovely. For me to entreat of[86] the one, being a novice, or to discourse of the other, being a truant, I may well make you weary but never the wiser, and give you occasion rather to laugh at my rashness than to like my reasons. Yet I care the less to excuse my boldness to you who were the cause of my blindness. And since I am at mine own choice either to talk of love or of learning, I had rather for this time be deemed an unthrift in rejecting profit than a Stoic in renouncing pleasure.

'It hath been a question often disputed, but never determined, whether the qualities of the mind or the composition of the man cause women most to like, or whether beauty or wit move men most to love. Certes, by how much the more the mind is to be preferred before the body, by so much the more the graces of the one are to be preferred before the gifts of the other; which, if it be so that the contemplation of the inward quality ought to be respected more than the view of the outward beauty, then doubtless women either do or should love those best whose virtue is best, not measuring the deformed man with the reformed mind. The foul toad hath a fair stone in his head, the fine gold is found in the filthy earth, the sweet kernel lieth in the hard shell. Virtue is harboured in the heart of him that most men esteem misshapen. Contrariwise, if we respect more the outward shape than the inward habit – good God, into how many mischiefs do we fall! Into what blindness are we led! Do we not commonly see that in painted pots is hidden the deadliest poison, that in the greenest grass is the greatest serpent, in the clearest water the ugliest toad? Doth not experience teach us that in the most curious[87] sepulchre are enclosed rotten bones, that the cypress tree beareth a fair leaf but no fruit, that the estridge[88] carrieth fair feathers but rank flesh? How frantic are those lovers which are carried away with the gay glistering of the fine face, the beauty whereof is parched with the summer's blaze and chipped with the winter's blast,

---

[85] *list*] wish   [86] *entreat of*] discuss   [87] *curious*] elaborately constructed
[88] *estridge*] ostrich

21

which is of so short continuance that it fadeth before one perceive it flourish, of so small profit that it poisoneth those that possess it, of so little value with the wise that they account it a delicate bait with a deadly hook, a sweet panther with a devouring paunch, a sour poison in a silver pot.

'Here I could enter into discourse of such fine dames as being in love with their own looks make such coarse account of their passionate lovers; for commonly, if they be adorned with beauty, they be so strait-laced and made so high in the instep[89] that they disdain them most that most desire them. It is a world[90] to see the doting of their lovers and their dealing with them, the revealing of whose subtle trains would cause me to shed tears and you, gentlewomen, to shut your modest ears. Pardon me, gentlewomen, if I unfold every wile[91] and and show every wrinkle of women's disposition. Two things do they cause their servants to vow unto them, secrecy and sovereignty, the one to conceal their enticing sleights, by the other to assure themselves of their only service. Again – but ho there! If I should have waded any further and sounded the depth of their deceit, I should either have procured your displeasure or incurred the suspicion of fraud, either armed you to practise the like subtlety or accused myself of perjury. But I mean not to offend your chaste minds with the rehearsal of their unchaste manners, whose ears I perceive to glow, and hearts to be grieved, at that which I have already uttered; not that amongst you there be any such, but that in your sex there should be any such.

'Let not gentlewomen, therefore, make too much of their painted sheath,[92] let them not be so curious in their own conceit,[93] or so currish to their loyal lovers. When the black crow's foot shall appear in their eye, or the black ox tread on their foot, when their beauty shall be like the blasted rose, their wealth wasted, their bodies worn, their faces wrinkled, their fingers crooked, who will like of them in their age, who loved none in their youth? If you will be cherished when you be old, be courteous while you be

[89] *high in the instep*] proud   [90] *It is a world*] it is a marvel
[91] *Pardon . . . wile*] excuse me, ladies if I do not reveal every stratagem
[92] *sheath*] body   [93] *curious in their own conceit*] exquisite in their own imaginations

young; if you look for comfort in your hoary hairs, be not coy when you have your golden locks; if you would be embraced in the waning of your bravery, be not squeamish in the waxing of your beauty; if you desire to be kept like the roses when they have lost their colour, smell sweet as the rose doth in the bud; if you would be tasted for old wine, be in the mouth a pleasant grape – so shall you be cherished for your courtesy, comforted for your honesty, embraced for your amity, so shall you be preserved with the sweet rose, and drunk with the pleasant wine.

'Thus far I am bold, gentlewomen, to counsel those that be coy, that they weave not the web of their own woe, nor spin the thread of their own thraldom by their own overthwartness.[94] And seeing we are even in the bowels of love, it shall not be amiss to examine whether man or woman be soonest allured, whether be most constant the male or the female. And in this point I mean not to be mine own carver, lest I should seem either to pick a thank[95] with men, or a quarrel with women. If, therefore, it might stand with your pleasure, Mistress Lucilla, to give your censure, I would take the contrary; for sure I am though your judgement be sound, yet affection[96] will shadow it.'

Lucilla, seeing his pretence, thought to take advantage of his large proffer, unto whom she said: 'Gentleman, in mine opinion women are to be won with every wind, in whose sex there is neither force to withstand the assaults of love, neither constancy to remain faithful. And because your discourse hath hitherto bred delight, I am loath to hinder you in the sequel of your devices.'

Euphues, perceiving himself to be taken napping, answered as followeth: 'Mistress Lucilla, if you speak as you think, these gentlewomen present have little cause to thank you; if you cause me to commend women, my tale will be accounted a mere trifle, and your words the plain truth. Yet knowing promise to be debt, I will pay it with performance. And I would the gentlemen here present were as ready to credit my proof as the gentlewomen are willing to hear their own praises; or I as able to overcome as Mistress Lucilla would be content to be overthrown. Howsoever the matter

[94] *thraldom / overthwartness*] servitude / cross-grained nature   [95] *pick a thank*] seek to ingratiate myself with   [96] *affection*] bias

23

shall fall out, I am of the surer side: for if my reasons be weak, then is our sex strong; if forcible, then your judgement feeble; if I find truth on my side, I hope I shall, for my wages, win the good will of women; if I want proof, then, gentlewomen, of necessity you must yield to men. But to the matter.

'Touching the yielding to love, albeit their hearts seem tender, yet they harden them like the stone of Sicilia,[97] the which the more it is beaten the harder it is; for being framed as it were of the perfection of men, they be free from all such cogitations as may any way provoke them to uncleanness,[98] insomuch as they abhor the light love of youth which is grounded upon lust and dissolved upon every light occasion. When they see the folly of men turn to fury, their delight to doting, their affection to frenzy; when they see them as it were pine in pleasure, and to wax pale through their own peevishness; their suits, their service, their letters, their labours, their loves, their lives seem to them so odious that they harden their hearts against such concupiscence, to the end they might convert them from rashness to reason, from such lewd disposition to honest discretion. Hereof it cometh that men accuse women of cruelty because they themselves want civility, they account them full of wiles in not yielding to their wickedness, faithless for resisting their filthiness. But I had almost forgot myself –. You shall pardon me, Mistress Lucilla, for this time, if this abruptly I finish my discourse. It is neither for want of good will, or lack of proof, but that I feel in myself such alteration that I can scarcely utter one word. Ah Euphues, Euphues!'

The gentlewomen were struck into such a quandary with this sudden change that they all changed colour. But Euphues, taking Philautus by the hand, and giving the gentlewomen thanks for their patience and his repast, bade them all farewell and went immediately to his chamber.

But Lucilla, who now began to fry in the flames of love, all the company being departed to their lodgings, entered into these terms and contrarieties:[99] 'Ah wretched wench Lucilla, how art thou perplexed! What a doubtful fight dost thou feel betwixt faith

---

[97]   *stone of Sicilia*] noted by Pliny for making good whetstones
[98]   *uncleanness*] impurity   [99]   *contrarieties*] opposing arguments

and fancy, hope and fear, conscience and concupiscence! O my Euphues, little dost thou know the sudden sorrow that I sustain for thy sweet sake, whose wit hath bewitched me, whose rare qualities have deprived me of mine old quality, whose courteous behaviour without curiosity,[100] whose comely feature without fault, whose filed[101] speech without fraud hath wrapped me in this misfortune. And canst thou, Lucilla, be so light of love in forsaking Philautus to fly to Euphues? Canst thou prefer a stranger before thy countryman, a starter[102] before thy companion? Why Euphues doth perhaps desire my love, but Philautus hath deserved it. Why Euphues' feature is worthy as good as I, but Philautus his faith is worthy a better. Aye, but the latter love is most fervent; aye, but the first ought to be most faithful. Aye, but Euphues hath greater perfection; aye, but Philautus hath deeper affection.

'Ah fond wench, dost thou think Euphues will deem thee constant to him, when thou hast been unconstant to his friend? Weenest thou[103] that he will have no mistrust of thy faithfulness, when he hath had trial of thy fickleness? Will he have no doubt of thine honour, when thou thyself callest thine honesty in question? Yes, yes, Lucilla, well doth he know that the glass once crazed will with the least clap[104] be cracked, that the cloth which staineth with milk will soon lose his colour with vinegar, that the eagle's wing will waste the feather as well of the phoenix as of the pheasant,[105] that she that hath been faithless to one will never be faithful to any.

'But can Euphues convince me of fleeting, seeing for his sake I break my fidelity? Can he condemn me of disloyalty, when he is the only cause of my disliking? May he justly condemn me of treachery, who hath this testimony as trial of my good will? Doth not he remember that the broken bone once set together is stronger than ever it was; that the greatest blot is taken off with the pumice; that though the spider poison the fly, she cannot infect the bee;

---

[100] *curiosity*] over preciseness [101] *filed*] polished [102] *starter*] runaway [103] *weenest thou*] do you think [104] *clap*] knock, bang [105] *eagle's wing . . . pheasant*] Eagles' feathers were believed to destroy those of other birds if placed among them.

that although I have been light to Philautus, yet I may be lovely to Euphues? It is not my desire but his deserts that moveth my mind to this choice; neither the want of the like good will in Philautus, but the lack of the like good qualities that removeth my fancy from the one to the other.

'For as the bee that gathereth honey out of the weed when she espieth the fair flower flieth to the sweetest; or as the kind[106] spaniel though he hunt after birds yet forsakes them to retrieve the partridge; or as we commonly feed on beef hungerly at the first, yet seeing the quail more dainty change our diet; so I, although I loved Philautus for his good properties, yet seeing Euphues to excel him I ought by nature to like him better. By so much the more, therefore, my change is to be excused, by how much the more my choice is excellent; and by so much the less I am to be condemned, by how much the more Euphues is to be commended. Is not the diamond of more value than the ruby because he is of more virtue? Is not the emerald preferred before the sapphire for his wonderful property? Is not Euphues more praiseworthy than Philautus being more witty?

'But fie, Lucilla, why dost thou flatter thyself in thine own folly? Canst thou feign Euphues thy friend, whom by thine own words thou hast made thy foe? Didst not thou accuse women of inconstancy? Didst not thou account them easy to be won? Didst not thou condemn them of weakness? What sounder argument can he have against thee than thine own answer; what better proof than thine own speech; what greater trial than thine own talk? If thou hast belied women, he will judge thee unkind;[107] if thou have revealed the truth, he must needs think thee unconstant; if he perceive thee to be won with a nut, he will imagine that thou wilt be lost with an apple; if he find thee wanton before thou be wooed, he will guess thou wilt be wavering when thou art wedded.

'But suppose that Euphues love thee, that Philautus leave thee, will thy father, thinkest thou, give thee liberty to live after thine own lust? Will he esteem him worthy to inherit his possessions whom he accounteth unworthy to enjoy thy person? Is it like that

[106] *kind*] true-bred   [107] *unkind*] unnatural

26

he will match thee in marriage with a stranger, with a Grecian, with a mean man? Aye, but what knoweth my father whether he be wealthy, whether his revenues be able to countervail my father's lands, whether his birth be noble, yea or no? Can anyone make doubt of his gentle blood that seeth his gentle conditions? Can his honour be called into question whose honesty is so great? Is he to be thought thriftless who in all qualities of the mind is peerless? No, no, the tree is known by his fruit, the gold by his touch,[108] the son by the sire. And as the soft wax receiveth whatsoever print be in the seal and showeth no other impression, so the tender babe, being sealed with his father's gifts, representeth his image most lively.

'But were I once certain of Euphues' good will I would not so superstitiously account of my father's ill will. Albeit I can no way quench the coals of desire with forgetfulness, yet will I rake them up in the ashes of modesty; seeing I dare not discover my love for maidenly shamefastness,[109] I will dissemble it till time I have opportunity. And I hope so to behave myself, as Euphues shall think me his own, and Philautus persuade himself I am none but his. But I would to God Euphues would repair hither, that the sight of him might mitigate some part of my martyrdom.'

She, having thus discoursed with herself her own miseries, cast herself on the bed. And there let her lie, and return we to Euphues – who was so caught in the gin[110] of folly that he neither could comfort himself nor durst ask counsel of his friend, suspecting that which indeed was true that Philautus was co-rival with him and cockmate[111] with Lucilla. Amidst, therefore, these his extremities, between hope and fear, he uttered these or the like speeches:

'What is he, Euphues, that knowing thy wit and seeing thy folly, but will rather punish thy lewdness than pity thy heaviness? Was there ever any so fickle so soon to be allured; any ever so faithless to deceive his friend; ever any so foolish to bathe himself in his own misfortune? Too true it is that as the sea-crab swimmeth

---

[108] *gold . . . touch*] A reference to the practice of testing gold by rubbing the metal on a touchstone.   [109] *discover / shamefastness*] reveal / modesty
[110] *gin*] trap   [111] *cockmate*] intimate

always against the stream, so wit always striveth against wisdom; and as the bee is oftentimes hurt with her own honey, so is wit not seldom plagued with his own conceit.[112]

'O ye gods, have ye ordained for every malady a medicine, for every sore a salve, for every pain a plaster, leaving only love remediless? Did ye deem[113] no man so mad to be entangled with desire, or thought ye them worthy to be tormented that were so misled? Have ye dealt more favourably with brute beasts than with reasonable creatures? The filthy sow when she is sick eateth the sea-crab and is immediately recured; the tortoise having tasted the viper sucketh *Origanum* and is quickly revived; the bear ready to pine licketh up the ants and is recovered; the dog having surfeited to procure his vomit eateth grass and findeth remedy; the hart being pierced with the dart runneth out of hand to the herb *Dictanum* and is healed. And can men by no herb, by no art, by no way procure a remedy for the impatient disease of love? Ah well I perceive that love is not unlike the fig-tree, whose fruit is sweet, whose root is more bitter than the claw of a bittern;[114] or like the apple in Persia, whose blossom savoureth like honey, whose bud is more sour than gall.

'But oh – impiety! Oh – broad blasphemy against the heavens! Wilt thou be so impudent, Euphues, to accuse the gods of iniquity? No, fond fool, no! Neither is it forbidden us by the gods to love, by whose divine providence we are permitted to live, neither do we want remedies to recure our maladies,[115] but reason to use the means. But why go I about to hinder the course of love with the discourse of law? Hast thou not read, Euphues, that he that loppeth the vine causeth it to spread fairer; that he that stoppeth the stream forceth it to swell higher; that he that casteth water on the fire in the smith's forge maketh it to flame fiercer? Even so, he that seeketh by counsel to moderate his overlashing affections increaseth his own misfortune.

'Ah my Lucilla, would thou wert either less fair, or I more fortunate; either I wiser, or thou milder; either would I were out of

---

[112] *conceit*] device   [113] *deem*] judge   [114] *bittern*] a marsh bird, eaten until recent times. The pun is more pointed in the original which reads 'bitter', the more common form of the name in the sixteenth-century.
[115] *want . . . maladies*] lack cures to treat our illnesses

this mad mood, either I would we were both of one mind. But how should she be persuaded of my loyalty that yet had never one simple proof of my love? Will she not rather imagine me to be entangled with her beauty than with her virtue; that my fancy being so lewdly chained at the first will be as lightly changed at the last; that there is nothing which is permanent that is violent? Yes, yes, she must needs conjecture so, although it be nothing so; for by how much the more my affection cometh on the sudden, by so much the less will she think it certain. The rattling thunderbolt hath but his clap, the lightning but his flash; and as they both come in a moment, so do they both end in a minute.

'Aye but, Euphues, hath she not heard also that the dry touchwood[116] is kindled with lime; that the greatest mushroom groweth in one night; that the fire quickly burneth the flax;[117] that love easily entereth into the sharp wit without resistance, and is harboured there without repentance? If, therefore, the gods have endowed her with as much bounty as beauty, if she have no less wit than she hath comeliness, certes,[118] she will neither conceive sinisterly of my sudden suit, neither be coy to receive me into her service, neither suspect me of lightness in yielding so lightly, neither reject me disdainfully for loving so hastily.

'Shall I not then hazard my life to obtain my love, and deceive Philautus to receive Lucilla? Yes, Euphues, where love beareth sway, friendship can have no show. As Philautus brought me for his shadow the last supper, so will I use him for my shadow till I have gained his saint. And canst thou, wretch, be false to him that is faithful to thee? Shall his courtesy be cause of thy cruelty? Wilt thou violate the league of faith to inherit the land of folly? Shall affection be of more force than friendship, love than law, lust than loyalty? Knowest thou not that he that loseth his honesty hath nothing else to lose?

'Tush, the case is light where reason taketh place; to love and to live well is not granted to Jupiter.[119] Whoso is blinded with the

---

[116] *touchwood*] easily lit wood used for kindling   [117] *flax*] material used for candle wicks   [118] *certes*] assuredly   [119] *case . . . Jupiter*] both proverbial. (i) The grief is slight which is capable of being eased by good counsel. (ii) The gods themselves behave badly when in love.

caul[120] of beauty discerneth no colour of honesty. Did not Gyges cut Candaules a coat by his own measure; did not Paris, though he were a welcome guest to Menelaus, serve his host a slippery prank?[121] If Philautus had loved Lucilla he would never have suffered Euphues to have seen her. Is it not the prey that enticeth the thief to rifle;[122] is it not the pleasant bait that causeth the fleetest fish to bite; is it not a byword amongst us that gold maketh an honest man an ill man? Did Philautus account Euphues too simple to decipher beauty, or superstitious[123] not to desire it? Did he deem him a saint in rejecting fancy, or a sot in not discerning? Thought he him a Stoic that he would not be moved, or a stock that he could not?

'Well, well, seeing the wound that bleedeth inward is most dangerous, that the fire kept close burneth most furious, that the oven dammed up baketh soonest, that sores having no vent fester inwardly, it is high time to unfold my secret love to my secret friend. Let Philautus behave himself never so craftily, he shall know that it must be a wily mouse that shall breed in the cat's ear; and because I resemble him in wit, I mean a little to dissemble with him in wiles.

'But, O my Lucilla, if thy heart be made of that stone which may be mollified only with blood,[124] would I had sipped of that river in Caria which turneth those that drink of it to stones. If thine ears be anointed with the oil of Syria that bereaveth hearing, would mine eyes had been rubbed with the syrup of the cedar tree which taketh away sight.'

Euphues having thus talked with himself, Philautus entered the chamber; and finding him so worn and wasted with continual mourning, neither joying in his meat nor rejoicing in his friend, with watery eyes uttered this speech:

[120] *caul*] veil-like membrane   [121] *Gyges . . . prank*] instances of betrayal motivated by lust. Gyges killed King Candaules and married his wife, having been force to spy on the latter's beauty. Paris abducted the wife of Menelaus having been entertained at the latter's court.   [122] *rifle*] rob
[123] *superstitious*] governed by religious scruples   [124] *stone . . . blood*] the diamond. One of its many fabulous properties is its capacity to be softened by blood.

'Friend and fellow, as I am not ignorant of thy present weakness, so I am not privy of the cause; and although I suspect many things, yet can I assure myself of no one thing. Therefore, my good Euphues, for these doubts and dumps of mine either remove the cause or reveal it. Thou hast hitherto found me a cheerful companion in thy mirth, and now shalt thou find me as careful[125] with thee in thy moan. If altogether thou mayest not be cured, yet mayest thou be comforted. If there be anything that either by my friends may be procured or by my life attained, that may either heal thee in part or help thee in all, I protest to thee by the name of a friend that it shall rather be gotten with the loss of my body, than lost by getting a kingdom. Thou hast tried me, therefore trust me; thou hast trusted me in many things, therefore try me in this one thing. I never yet failed, and now I will not faint. Be bold to speak and blush not; thy sore is not so angry but I can salve it, thy wound not so deep but I can search it, thy grief not so great but I can ease it. If it be ripe[126] it shall be lanced, if it be broken it shall be tainted,[127] be it never so desperate it shall be cured. Rise, therefore, Euphues, and take heart at grass.[128] Younger thou shalt never be: pluck up thy stomach. If love itself have stung thee, it shall not stifle thee; though thou be enamoured of some lady, thou shalt not be enchanted. They that begin to pine of a consumption without delay preserve themselves with cullises;[129] he that feeleth his stomach enflamed with heat, cooleth it eftsoons with conserves;[130] delays breed dangers; nothing so perilous as procrastination.'

Euphues, hearing this comfort and friendly counsel, dissembled his sorrowing heart with a smiling face, answering him forthwith as followeth: 'True it is, Philautus, that he which toucheth the nettle tenderly is soonest stung, that the fly which playeth with the fire is singed in the flame, that he that dallieth with women is drawn to his woe. And as the adamant draweth the heavy iron, the harp the fleet dolphin, so beauty allureth the

---

[125] *careful*] full of care   [126] *ripe*] ready to burst   [127] *tainted*] anointed
[128] *take . . . grass*] revive your spirits (common expression of uncertain origin)
[129] *cullises*] thick broths   [130] *eftsoons / conserves*] immediately / medicinal preserves

chaste mind to love, and the wisest wit to lust. The example whereof I would it were no less profitable than the experience to me is like to be perilous. The vine watered with wine is soon withered, the blossom in the fattest ground is quickly blasted, the goat the fatter she is the less fertile she is; yea, man the more witty he is the less happy[131] he is. So it is, Philautus (for why should I conceal it from thee of whom I am to take counsel?) that since my last and first being with thee at the house of Ferardo, I have felt such a furious battle in mine own body as, if it be not speedily repressed by policy, it will carry my mind (the grand captain in this fight) into endless captivity. Ah Livia, Livia, thy courtly grace without coyness, thy blazing beauty without blemish, thy courteous demeanour without curiosity,[132] thy sweet speech savoured with wit, thy comely mirth tempered with modesty, thy chaste looks yet lovely, thy sharp taunts yet pleasant, have given me such a check that, sure I am, at the next view of thy virtues I shall take the mate.[133] And taking it not of a pawn but of a prince, the loss is to be accounted the less. And though they be commonly in a great choler that receive the mate, yet would I willingly take every minute ten mates to enjoy Livia for my loving mate.

'Doubtless, if ever she herself have been scorched with the flames of desire, she will be ready to quench the coals with courtesy in another; if ever she have been attached of[134] love, she will rescue him that is drenched in desire; if ever she have been taken with the fever of fancy, she will help his ague who by a quotidian fit[135] is converted into frenzy. Neither can there be under so delicate a hue lodged deceit, neither in so beautiful a mould[136] a malicious mind. True it is that the disposition of the mind followeth the composition of the body; how then can she be in mind any way imperfect who in body is perfect every way?

'I know my success will be good, but I know not how to have access to my goddess; neither do I want courage to discover my

---

[131] *happy*] fortunate   [132] *curiosity*] undue nicety   [133] *take the mate*] All early eds before 1631 read 'take thee mate'. The sense, however, is clearly not 'take you as my partner' but 'be checkmated by you'. See the chess imagery of the following lines.   [134] *attached of*] seized by   [135] *quotidian fit*] an intermittent fever, recurring daily   [136] *mould*] bodily form

32

love to my friend, but some colour[137] to cloak my coming to the house of Ferardo. For if they be in Naples as jealous as they be in the other parts of Italy, then it behoveth me to walk circumspectly, and to forge some cause for mine often coming. If, therefore, Philautus, thou canst set but this feather to mine arrow, thou shalt see me shoot so near that thou wilt account me for a cunning archer. And verily if I had not loved thee well, I would have swallowed mine own sorrow in silence, knowing that in love nothing is so dangerous as to participate the means thereof to another, and that two may keep counsel if one be away.[138] I am, therefore, enforced perforce to challenge that courtesy at thy hands which erst[139] thou didst promise with thy heart, the performance whereof shall bind me to Philautus, and prove thee faithful to Euphues.'

Philautus, thinking all to be gold that glistered and all to be gospel that Euphues uttered, answered his forged gloze with this friendly close:[140] 'In that thou hast made me privy to thy purpose, I will not conceal my practice; in that thou cravest my aid, assure thyself I will be the finger next the thumb; insomuch as thou shalt never repent thee of the one, or of the other. Concerning Livia, though she be fair yet is she not so amiable as my Lucilla, whose servant I have been the term of three years – but lest comparisons should seem odious, chiefly where both the parties be without comparison, I will omit that. And seeing that we had both rather be talking with them than tattling of them, we will immediately go to them. And truly, Euphues, I am not a little glad that I shall have thee not only a comfort in my life, but also a companion in my love. As thou hast been wise in thy choice, so I hope thou shalt be fortunate in thy chance. Livia is a wench of more wit than beauty, Lucilla of more beauty than wit; both of more honesty than honour, and yet both of such honour as in all Naples there is not one in birth to be compared with any of them both. How much, therefore, have we to rejoice in our choice.

---

137 *colour*] pretence   138 *two . . . away*] proverbial, implying that no one can be trusted with a secret   139 *erst*] formerly   140 *forged gloze /
friendly close*] deceitful eloquence / sympathetic response

'Touching our access, be thou secure. I will flap Ferardo in the mouth with some conceit,[141] and fill his old head so full of new fables that thou shalt rather be earnestly entreated to repair to his house, than evil entreated to leave it. As old men are very suspicious to mistrust everything, so are they very credulous to believe anything; the blind man doth eat many a fly.'

'Yea, but,' said Euphues, 'take heed, my Philautus, that thou thyself swallow not a gudgeon,'[142] which word Philautus did not mark until he had almost digested it.

'But,' said Philautus,[143] 'let us go devoutly to the shrine of our saints, there to offer our devotion.' To the which Euphues consented willingly, smiling to himself to see how he had brought Philautus into a fool's paradise.

Here you may see, gentlemen, the falsehood in fellowship, the fraud in friendship, the painted sheath with the leaden dagger, the fair words that make fools fain. But I will not trouble you with superfluous addition, unto whom I fear me I have been tedious with the bare discourse of this rude history.

Philautus and Euphues repaired to the house of Ferardo, where they found Mistress Lucilla and Livia, accompanied with other gentlewomen, neither being idle nor well employed, but playing at cards. But when Lucilla beheld Euphues she could scarcely contain herself from embracing him, had not womanly shamefastness, and Philautus his presence, stayed her wisdom. Euphues, on the other side, was fallen into such a trance that he had not the power either to succour himself, or salute the gentlewomen. At the last Lucilla began, as one that best might be bold, on this manner:

'Gentlemen, although your long absence gave me occasion to think that you disliked your late entertainment, yet your coming at the last hath cut off my former suspicion. And by so much the more you are welcome, by how much the more you were wished for. But you, gentleman,' (taking Euphues by the hand), 'were the rather wished for, for that your discourse being left unperfect

---

[141] *flap . . . conceit*] present Ferardo with some falsehood   [142] *swallow . . .a gudgeon*] take the bait, i.e. be deceived   [143] *Philautus*] All early editions read 'Euphues' but the next sentence makes plain that Philautus is the speaker.

caused us all to long (as women are wont for things that like them) to have an end thereof.'

Unto whom Philautus replied as followeth: 'Mistress Lucilla, though your courtesy made us nothing to doubt of our welcome, yet modesty caused us to pinch courtesy[144] who should first come. As for my friend, I think he was never wished for here so earnestly of any as of himself, whether it might be to renew his talk or to recant his sayings I cannot tell.'

But whilst he was yet speaking Ferardo entered, whom they all dutifully welcomed home; who, rounding Philautus in the ear, desired him to accompany him immediately without further pausing, protesting it should be as well for his preferment as for his own profit. Philautus consenting, Ferardo said to his daughter: 'Lucilla, the urgent affairs I have in hand will scarce suffer me to tarry with you one hour. Yet my return, I hope, will be so short that my absence shall not breed thy sorrow. In the mean season, I commit all things into thy custody, wishing thee to use thy accustomable courtesy. And seeing I must take Philautus with me, I will be so bold to crave you, gentleman (his friend), to supply his room, desiring you to take this hasty warning for a hearty welcome, and so to spend this time of mine absence in honest mirth. And thus I leave you.'

Philautus knew well the cause of this sudden departure, which was to redeem certain lands that were mortgaged in his father's time to the use of Ferardo; who on that condition had beforetime promised him his daughter in marriage. But return we to Euphues.

Euphues was surprised with such incredible joy at this strange event that he had almost swooned; for seeing his co-rival to be departed, and Ferardo to give him so friendly entertainment, doubted not in time to get the good will of Lucilla. Whom finding in place convenient without company, with a bold courage and comely gesture he began to assay her in this sort:

'Gentlewoman, my acquaintance being so little, I am afraid my credit will be less, for that they commonly are soonest believed that are best beloved, and they liked best whom we have known

---

[144] *pinch courtesy*] be over-punctilious about

longest. Nevertheless, the noble mind suspecteth no guile without cause, neither condemneth any wight[145] without proof. Having, therefore, notice of your heroical heart, I am the better persuaded of my good hap.[146]

'So it is, Lucilla, that coming to Naples but to fetch fire, as the byword is, not to make my place of abode,[147] I have found such flames that I can neither quench them with the water of free will, neither cool them with wisdom. For as the hop, the pole being never so high, groweth to the end, or as the dry beech kindled at the root never leaveth until it come to the top, or as one drop of poison disperseth itself into every vein, so affection having caught hold of my heart, and the sparkles of love kindled my liver,[148] will suddenly, though secretly, flame up into my head, and spread itself into every sinew. It is your beauty (pardon my abrupt boldness), lady, that hath taken every part of me prisoner, and brought me to this deep distress. But seeing women, when one praiseth them for their deserts, deem that he flattereth them to obtain his desire, I am here present to yield myself to such trial as your courtesy in this behalf shall require.

'Yet will you commonly object this to such as serve you and starve[149] to win your good will: that hot love is soon cold; that the bavin,[150] though it burn bright, is but a blaze; that scalding water, if it stand a while, turneth almost to ice; that pepper, though it be hot in the mouth, is cold in the maw;[151] that the faith of men, though it fry in their words, it freezeth in their works. Which things, Lucilla, albeit they be sufficient to reprove the lightness of some one, yet can it not convince every one of lewdness; neither ought the constancy of all to be brought in question through the subtlety of a few. For although the worm entereth almost into every wood, yet he eateth not the cedar tree; though the stone *Cylindrus* at every thunderclap roll from the hill, yet the

---

[145] *wight*] person [146] *hap*] fortune [147] *but to fetch fire . . . place of abode*] proverbial, to visit rather than to stay. Drawn from the practice of going to a neighbour's house to fetch live coals in order to light a fire. [148] *liver*] a traditional seat of the passions [149] *starve*] die (specifically to perish with cold) [150] *bavin*] bundle of brushwood [151] *maw*] stomach

pure sleek-stone mounteth at the noise; [152] though the rust fret the hardest steel, yet doth it not eat into the emerald; though Polypus change his hue, yet the *Salamander*[153] keepeth his colour; though Proteus transform himself into every shape, yet Pygmalion[154] retaineth his old form; though Aeneas were too fickle to Dido, yet Troilus was too faithful to Cressida; [155] though others seem counterfeit in their deeds, yet, Lucilla, persuade yourself that Euphues will be always current in his dealings.

'But as the true gold is tried by the touch, the pure flint by the stroke of the iron, so the loyal heart of the faithful lover is known by the trial of his lady. Of the which trial, Lucilla, if you shall account Euphues worthy, assure yourself he will be as ready to offer himself a sacrifice for your sweet sake, as yourself shall be willing to employ him in your service. Neither doth he desire to be trusted any way until he shall be tried every way, neither doth he crave credit at the first, but a good countenance till time[156] his desire shall be made manifest by his deserts. Thus not blinded by light affection, but dazzled with your rare perfection, and boldened by your exceeding courtesy, I have unfolded mine entire love; desiring you, having so good leisure, to give so friendly an answer as I may receive comfort and you commendation.'

Lucilla, although she were contented to hear this desired discourse, yet did she seem to be somewhat displeased. And truly I know not whether it be peculiar to that sex to dissemble with those whom they most desire, or whether by craft they have learned outwardly to loathe that which inwardly they most love. Yet wisely did she cast this in her head, that if she should yield at the first assault he would think her a light huswife,[157] if she

---

[152] *stone Cylindrus . . . noise*] No source has been found for these comparisons. A sleek-stone is used for polishing. [153] *Polypus . . . Salamander*] mythological creatures, the former a fish reputed to adapt its colour to its environment, the latter thought to be capable of living, unchanged, in fire. [154] *Proteus . . . Pygmalion*] mythological figures, the former able to transform himself to any shape, the latter a sculptor associated through his constancy with the immutability of his medium. [155] *Aeneas . . . Cressida*] archetypes of unfaithful and faithful lovers. Aeneas, founder of Rome, deserted the Carthaginian queen, Dido; Troilus, a Trojan prince, was faithful to Cressida who deserted him for Diomedes. [156] *till time*] until such time as [157] *huswife*] hussy

should reject him scornfully a very haggard. Minding, therefore, that he should neither take hold of her promise, neither unkindness of her preciseness, she fed him indifferently[158] with hope and despair, reason and affection, life and death. Yet in the end, arguing wittily upon certain questions, they fell to such agreement as poor Philautus would not have agreed unto if he had been present, yet always keeping the body undefiled. And thus she replied:

'Gentleman, as you may suspect me of idleness in giving ear to your talk, so may you convince me of lightness in answering such toys. Certes, as you have made mine ears glow at the rehearsal of your love, so have you galled my heart with the remembrance of your folly. Though you came to Naples as a stranger, yet were you welcome to my father's house as a friend. And can you then so much transgress the bounds of honour (I will not say of honesty) as to solicit a suit more sharp to me than death? I have hitherto, God be thanked, lived without suspicion of lewdness, and shall I now incur the danger of sensual liberty? What hope can you have to obtain my love, seeing yet I could never afford you a good look? Do you, therefore, think me easily enticed to the bent of your bow, because I was easily entreated to listen to your late discourse; or seeing me (as finely you gloze) to excel all other in beauty, did you deem that I would exceed all other in beastliness?

'But yet I am not angry, Euphues, but in an agony; for who is she that will not fret or fume with one that loveth her – if this love to delude me be not dissembled? It is that which causeth me most to fear; not that my beauty is unknown to myself, but that commonly we poor wenches are deluded through light belief, and ye men are naturally inclined craftily to lead your life. When the fox preacheth, the geese perish; the crocodile shroudeth greatest treason under most pitiful tears; in a kissing mouth there lieth a galling mind. You have made so large proffer of your service, and so fair promises of fidelity, that were I not over chary of mine honesty, you would inveigle me to shake hands with chastity. But, certes, I will either lead a virgin's life in earth (though I lead

---

158 *indifferently*] even-handedly

38

apes in hell),[159] or else follow thee rather than thy gifts. Yet am I neither so precise[160] to refuse thy proffer, neither so peevish to disdain thy good-will; so excellent always are the gifts which are made acceptable by the virtue of the giver.

'I did at the first entrance discern thy love, but yet dissemble it. Thy wanton glances, thy scalding sighs, thy loving signs caused me to blush for shame, and to look wan for fear, lest they should be perceived of any. These subtle shifts, these painted practices (if I were to be won) would soon wean me from the teat of Vesta to the toys of Venus. Besides this, thy comely grace, thy rare qualities, thy exquisite perfection were able to move a mind half mortified[161] to transgress the bonds of maidenly modesty. But God shield, Lucilla, that thou shouldst be so careless of thine honour as to commit the state thereof to a stranger. Learn thou by me, Euphues, to despise things that be amiable, to forgo delightful practices; believe me, it is piety to abstain from pleasure.

'Thou art not the first that hath solicited this suit, but the first that goeth about to seduce me; neither discernest thou more than other, but darest more than any; neither hast thou more art to discover thy meaning, but more heart to open thy mind. But thou preferrest me before thy lands, thy livings, thy life; thou offerest thyself a sacrifice for my security; thou profferest me the whole and only sovereignty of thy service: truly I were very cruel and hard-hearted if I should not love thee. Hard-hearted albeit I am not, but truly love thee I cannot, whom I doubt to be my lover. Moreover I have not been used to the court of Cupid, wherein there be more sleights than there be hares in Athos, than bees in Hybla, than stars in heaven. Besides this, the common people here in Naples are not only both very suspicious of other men's matters and manners, but also very jealous over other men's children and maidens. Either, therefore, dissemble thy fancy or desist from thy folly. But why shouldest thou desist from the one, seeing thou canst cunningly dissemble the other? My father is now gone to Venice, and as I am uncertain of his return so am I not privy to the cause of his travel. But yet is he so from hence that he

---

[159] *lead apes in hell*] the proverbial fate of old maids   [160] *precise*] over-scrupulous   [161] *half-mortified*] half dead to human feeling

39

seeth me in his absence. Knowest thou not, Euphues, that kings have long arms and rulers large reaches? Neither let this comfort thee, that at his departure he deputed thee in Philautus' place. Although my face cause him to mistrust my loyalty, yet my faith enforceth him to give me this liberty; though he be suspicious of my fair hue, yet is he secure of my firm honesty.

'But alas, Euphues, what truth can there be found in a traveller, what stay in a stranger, whose words and bodies both watch but for a wind, whose feet are ever fleeting, whose faith plighted on the shore is turned to perjury when they hoist sail? Who more traitorous to Phyllis than Demophon, yet he a traveller? Who more perjured to Dido than Aeneas, and he a stranger? Both these queens, both they caitiffs. Who more false to Ariadne than Theseus, yet he a sailor? Who more fickle to Medea than Jason,[162] yet he a starter? Both these daughters to great princes, both they unfaithful of promises. Is it then likely that Euphues will be faithful to Lucilla being in Naples but a sojourner?

'I have not yet forgotten the invective (I can no otherwise term it) which thou madest against beauty, saying it was a deceitful bait with a deadly hook, and a sweet poison in a painted pot. Canst thou then be so unwise to swallow the bait which will breed thy bane; to swill the drink that will expire thy date; to desire the wight that will work thy death? But it may be that with the scorpion thou canst feed on the earth, or with the quail and roebuck be fat with poison, or with beauty live in all bravery.

'I fear me thou hast the stone *Continens* about thee, which is named of the contrary; that though thou pretend faith in thy words, thou devisest fraud in thy heart; that though thou seem to prefer love, thou art inflamed with lust. And what for that? Though thou have eaten the seeds of rocket[163] which breed incontinency, yet have I chewed the leaf cress which maintaineth modesty. Though thou bear in thy bosom the herb Araxa, most noisome[164] to virginity, yet have I the stone that groweth in the mount Tmolus, the upholder of chastity.

---

[162] *Demophon . . . Jason*] all travellers who failed those who fell in love with them in the course of their journeys.   [163] *rocket*] plant used in salads
[164] *noisome*] harmful

'You may, gentleman, account me for a cold prophet, thus hastily to divine of your disposition. Pardon me, Euphues, if in love I cast beyond the moon, which bringeth us women to endless moan. Although I myself were never burnt, whereby I should dread the fire, yet the scorching of others in the flames of fancy warneth me to beware; though I as yet never tried any faithless, whereby I should be fearful, yet have I read of many that have been perjured, which causeth me to be careful; though I am able to convince none by proof, yet am I enforced to suspect one upon probabilities. Alas, we silly[165] souls which have neither wit to decipher the wiles of men, nor wisdom to dissemble our affection, neither craft to train in young lovers, neither courage to withstand their encounters, neither discretion to discern their doubling, neither hard hearts to reject their complaints – we, I say, are soon enticed being by nature simple, and easily entangled being apt to receive the impression of love. But alas, it is both common and lamentable to behold simplicity entrapped by subtlety, and those that have most might to be infected with most malice. The spider weaveth a fine web to hang the fly, the wolf weareth a fair face to devour the lamb, the merlin striketh at the partridge, the eagle often snappeth at the fly, men are always laying baits for women which are the weaker vessels. But as yet I could never hear man by such snares to entrap man. For true it is, that men themselves have by use observed, that it must be a hard winter when one wolf eateth another. I have read that the bull being tied to the fig-tree loseth his strength; that the whole herd of deer stand at the gaze if they smell a sweet apple; that the dolphin by the sound of music is brought to the shore. And then no marvel it is that if the fierce bull be tamed with the fig-tree, if that women (being as weak as sheep) be overcome with a fig; if the wild deer be caught with an apple, that the tame damsel is won with a blossom; if the fleet dolphin be allured with harmony, that women be entangled with the melody of men's speech, fair promises, and solemn protestations.

'But folly it were for me to mark their mischiefs. Sith I am neither able, neither they willing, to amend their manners, it becometh

---

[165] *silly*] simple

me rather to show what our sex should do, than to open what yours doth. And seeing I cannot by reason restrain your importunate suit, I will by rigour done on myself cause you to refrain the means. I would to God Ferardo were in this point like to Lysander,[166] which would not suffer his daughters to wear gorgeous apparel, saying it would rather make them common than comely. I would it were in Naples a law, which was a custom in Egypt, that women should always go barefoot, to the intent they might keep themselves always at home, that they should be ever like to the snail which hath ever his house on his head. I mean so to mortify myself that instead of silks I will wear sackcloth; for ouches[167] and bracelets, lear and caddis;[168] for the lute use the distaff; for the pen, the needle; for lovers' sonnets, David's psalms.

'But yet I am not so senseless altogether to reject your service; which if I were certainly assured to proceed of a simple mind, it should not receive so simple a reward.[169] And what greater trial can I have of thy simplicity and truth than thine own request which desireth a trial? Aye, but in the coldest flint there is hot fire; the bee that hath honey in her mouth hath a sting in her tail; the tree that beareth the sweetest fruit hath a sour sap; yea, the words of men though they seem smooth as oil, yet their hearts are as crooked as the stalk of ivy. I would not, Euphues, that thou shouldst condemn me of rigour, in that I seek to assuage thy folly by reason; but take this by the way that, although as yet I am disposed to like of none, yet whensoever I shall love any I will not forget thee. In the mean season account me thy friend, for thy foe I will never be.'

Euphues was brought into a great quandary and as it were a cold shivering to hear this new kind of kindness; such sweet meat, such sour sauce; such fair words, such faint promises; such hot love, such cold desire; such certain hope, such sudden change:

---

[166] *Lysander*] Spartan leader (d.395 BC) noted for his austerity
[167] *ouches*] brooches set with precious stones [168] *lear / caddis*] tape / coarse worsted binding (i.e. homely decorations) [169] *simple mind / simple a reward*] undesigning mind / poor a return

and stood like one that had looked on Medusa's head,[170] and so had been turned into a stone. Lucilla, seeing him in this pitiful plight and fearing he would take stand if the lure were not cast out,[171] took him by the hand and wringing[172] him softly, with a smiling countenance, began thus to comfort him: 'Methinks, Euphues, changing so your colour upon the sudden, you will soon change your copy.[173] Is your mind on your meat? A penny for your thought.'

'Mistress,' quoth he, 'if you would buy all my thoughts at that price, I should never be weary of thinking; but seeing it is too dear, read it, and take it for nothing.'

'It seems to me,' said she, 'that you are in some brown study what colours you might best wear for your lady.'

'Indeed, Lucilla, you level shrewdly at my thought by the aim of your own imagination. For you have given unto me a true-love's knot wrought of changeable silk, and you deem me that I am devising how I might have my colours changeable also that they might agree. But let this with such toys and devices pass. If it please you to command me any service, I am here ready to attend your leisure.'

'No service, Euphues, but that you keep silence until I have uttered my mind; and secrecy when I have unfolded my meaning.'

'If I should offend in the one I were too bold, if in the other too beastly.'

'Well then, Euphues,' said she, 'so it is that for the hope that I conceive of thy loyalty and the happy success that is like to ensue of this our love, I am content to yield thee the place in my heart which thou desirest and deservest above all other; which consent in me, if it may any ways breed thy contentation, sure I am that it will every way work my comfort. But as either thou tenderest mine honour or thine own safety, use such secrecy in this matter

---

[170] *Medusa's head*] mythological. The head of one of the gorgons, having the power to turn those who looked on it to stone. [171] *take stand . . . cast out*] image drawn from falconry. To remain in a state of arrested movement until attracted by a lure. [172] *wringing*] squeezing [173] *change your copy*] change your behaviour or course of action

that my father have no inkling hereof before I have framed his mind fit for our purpose. And though women have small force to overcome men by reason, yet have they good fortune to undermine them by policy. The soft drops of rain pierce the hard marble, many strokes overthrow the tallest oak, a silly woman in time may make such a breach into a man's heart as her tears may enter without resistance; then doubt not but I will so undermine mine old father as quickly I will enjoy my new friend. Tush, Philautus was liked for fashion sake, but never loved for fancy sake; and this I vow by the faith of a virgin and by the love I bear thee (for greater bands[174] to confirm my vow I have not) that my father shall sooner martyr me in the fire than marry me to Philautus. No, no, Euphues, thou only hast won me by love, and shalt only wear me by law; I force not[175] Philautus his fury so I may have Euphues his friendship, neither will I prefer his possessions before thy person, neither esteem better of his lands than of thy love. Ferardo shall sooner disinherit me of my patrimony than dishonour me in breaking my promise. It is not his great manors but thy good manners that shall make my marriage. In token of which my sincere affection, I give thee my hand in pawn and my heart for ever to be thy Lucilla.'

Unto whom Euphues answered in this manner: 'If my tongue were able to utter the joys that my heart hath conceived, I fear me though I be well beloved, yet I should hardly be believed. Ah my Lucilla, how much am I bound to thee, which preferest mine unworthiness before thy father's wrath, my happiness before thine own misfortune, my love before thine own life! How might I excel thee in courtesy, whom no mortal creature can exceed in constancy? I find it now for a settled truth, which erst I accounted for a vain talk, that the purple dye will never stain, that the pure civet[176] will never lose his savour, that the green laurel will never change his colour, that beauty can never be blotted with discourtesy. As touching secrecy in this behalf, assure thyself that I will not so much as tell it to myself. Command Euphues to run,

---

[174] *bands*] bonds   [175] *force not*] care not for   [176] *civet*] substance derived from the civet-cat, used in making perfumes

to ride, to undertake any exploit, be it never so dangerous, to hazard himself in any enterprise, be it never so desperate.'

As they were thus pleasantly conferring the one with the other,
Livia (whom Euphues made his stale)[177] entered into the parlour,
unto whom Lucilla spake in these terms: 'Dost thou not laugh,
Livia, to see my ghostly father keep me here so long at shrift?'

'Truly,' answered Livia, 'methinks that you smile at some
pleasant shift.[178] Either he is slow in enquiring of your faults, or
you slack in answering of his questions.'

And thus being supper time they all sat down, Lucilla well
pleased, no man better content than Euphues; who after his
repast, having no opportunity to confer with his lover, had small
lust to continue with the gentlewomen[179] any longer. Seeing,
therefore, he could frame no means to work his delight, he coined
an excuse to hasten his departure, promising the next morning to
trouble them again as a guest more bold than welcome, although
indeed he thought himself to be the better welcome in saying that
he would come.

But as Ferardo went in post,[180] so he returned in haste, having
concluded with Philautus that the marriage should immediately
be consummated, which wrought such a content in Philautus that
he was almost in an ecstacy through the extremity of his passions.
Such is the fulness and force of pleasure that there is nothing so
dangerous as the fruition. Yet knowing that delays bring dangers,
although he nothing doubted of Lucilla whom he loved, yet
feared he the fickleness of old men, which is always to be mis-
trusted. He urged, therefore, Ferardo to break with his daughter,
who, being willing to have the match made, was content incontinently[181] to procure the means. Finding, therefore, his daughter
at leisure, and having knowledge of her former love, spake to her
as followeth:

'Dear daughter, as thou hast long time lived a maiden, so now
thou must learn to be a mother; and as I have been careful to
bring thee up a virgin, so am I now desirous to make thee a wife.

---

[177] *stale*] decoy   [178] *shift*] device. Pun on 'shrift' (confession) in the
previous sentence).   [179] *gentlewomen*] 1578 edn reads 'gentlewoman'.
Corrected in later eds.   [180] *in post*] in a hurry   [181] *incontinently*]
without delay

45

Neither ought I in this matter to use any persuasions, for that maidens commonly nowadays are no sooner born but they begin to bride it; neither to offer any great portions, for that thou knowest thou shalt inherit all my possessions. Mine only care hath been hitherto to match thee with such an one as should be of good wealth able to maintain thee, of great worship able to compare with thee in birth, of honest conditions to deserve thy love, and an Italian-born to enjoy my lands. At the last I have found one answerable to my desire, a gentleman of great revenues, of a noble progeny, of honest behaviour, of comely personage, born and brought up in Naples – Philautus, thy friend as I guess, thy husband, Lucilla, if thou like it; neither canst thou dislike him who wanteth nothing that should cause thy liking, neither hath anything that should breed thy loathing. And surely I rejoice the more that thou shalt be linked to him in marriage whom thou hast loved as I hear being a maiden, neither can there any jars kindle between them where the minds be so united, neither any jealousy arise where love hath so long been settled.

'Therefore, Lucilla, to the end the desire of either of you may now be accomplished to the delight of you both, I am here come to finish the contract by giving hands, which you have already begun between yourselves by joining of hearts; that as God doth witness the one in your consciences, so the world may testify the other by your conversations. And therefore, Lucilla, make such answer to my request as may like me and satisfy thy friend.'

Lucilla, abashed with this sudden speech of her father, yet boldened by the love of her friend, with a comely bashfulness answered him in this manner:

'Reverend sir, the sweetness that I have found in the undefiled estate of virginity causeth me to loathe the sour sauce which is mixed with matrimony, and the quiet life which I have tried being a maiden maketh me to shun the cares that are always incident to a mother. Neither am I so wedded to the world that I should be moved with great possessions, neither so bewitched with wantonness that I should be enticed with any man's proportion,[182] neither (if I were so disposed) would I be so proud to

---

[182] *proportion*] shape

desire one of noble progeny, or so precise to choose one only in mine own country, for that commonly these things happen always to the contrary. Do we not see the noble to match with the base, the rich with the poor, the Italian oftentimes with the Portingale?[183] As love knoweth no laws, so it regardeth no conditions; as the lover maketh no pause where he liketh, so he maketh no conscience of these idle ceremonies.

'In that Philautus is the man that threateneth such kindness at my hands, and such courtesy at yours, that he should account me his wife before he woo me, certainly he is like, for me, to make his reckoning twice, because he reckoneth without his hostess.[184] And in this Philautus would either show himself of great wisdom to persuade, or me of great lightness to be allured: although the loadstone draw iron, yet can it not move gold; though the jet gather up the light straw, yet it cannot take up the pure steel; although Philautus think himself of virtue sufficient to win his lover, yet shall he not obtain Lucilla. I cannot but smile to hear that a marriage should be solomnised where never was any mention of assuring,[185] and that the wooing should be a day after the wedding. Certes, if when I looked merrily on Philautus he deemed it in the way of marriage, or if seeing me disposed to jest he took me in good earnest, then sure he might gather some presumption of my love, but no promise. But methinks it is good reason that I should be at mine own bridal, and not given in the church before I know the bridegroom.

'Therefore, dear father, in mine opinion, as there can be no bargain where both be not agreed, neither any indentures sealed where the one will not consent, so can there be no contract where both be not content, no banns asked lawfully where one of the parties forbiddeth them, no marriage made where no match was meant. But I will hereafter frame myself to be coy, seeing I am claimed for a wife because I have been courteous, and give myself to melancholy, seeing I am accounted won in that I have been merry. And if every gentleman be made of the metal that Philautus

---

[183] *Portingale*] Portuguese   [184] *to make his reckoning . . . hostess*] proverb drawn from inn-keeping. To recalculate because he has left the principal person involved out of account.   [185] *assuring*] betrothal

47

is, then I fear I shall be challenged of as many as I have used to company with, and be a common wife to all those that have commonly resorted hither.

'My duty therefore ever reserved, I here on my knees forswear Philautus for my husband, although I accept him for my friend. And seeing I shall hardly be induced ever to match with any, I beseech you, if by your fatherly love I shall be compelled, that I may match with such a one as both I may love and you may like.'

Ferardo, being a grave and wise gentleman, although he were throughly angry, yet he dissembled his fury to the end he might by craft discover her fancy. And whispering Philautus in the ear (who stood as though he had a flea in his ear),[186] desired him to keep silence until he had undermined her by subtlety, which Philautus having granted, Ferardo began to sift his daughter with this device:

'Lucilla, thy colour showeth thee to be in a great choler, and thy hot words bewray[187] thy heavy wrath; but be patient, seeing all my talk was only to try thee. I am neither so unnatural to wrest thee against thine own will, neither so malicious to wed thee to any against thine own liking; for well I know what jars, what jealousy, what strife, what storms ensue where the match is made rather by the compulsion of the parents than by consent of the parties. Neither do I like thee the less in that thou likest Philautus so little, neither can Philautus love thee the worse in that thou lovest thyself so well, wishing rather to stand to thy chance than to the choice of any other.

'But this grieveth me most, that thou art almost vowed to the vain order of the vestal virgins, despising, or at the least not desiring, the sacred bands of Juno her bed.[188] If thy mother had been of that mind when she was a maiden, thou hadst not now been born to be of this mind to be a virgin. Weigh with thyself what slender profit they bring to the commonwealth, what slight pleasure to themselves, what great grief to their parents, which

---

[186] *as though . . . ear*] as if he had heard something that had surprised and vexed him   [187] *bewray*] reveal   [188] *almost vowed . . . Juno her bed*] virtually commited to a life of chastity, rejecting the holy bonds of the goddess of married love

joy most in their offspring and desire most to enjoy the noble and blessed name of a grandfather. Thou knowest that the tallest ash is cut down for fuel because it beareth no good fruit, that the cow that gives no milk is brought to the slaughter, that the drone that gathereth no honey is contemned, that the woman that maketh herself barren by not marrying is accounted among the Grecian ladies worse than a carrion, as Homer reporteth. Therefore, Lucilla, if thou have any care to be a comfort to my hoary hairs, or a commodity to thy commonweal, frame thyself to that honourable estate of matrimony which was sanctified in Paradise, allowed of the Patriarchs, hallowed of the old Prophets, and commended of all persons.

'If thou like any, be not ashamed to tell it me, which only am to exhort thee, yea and as much as in me lieth to command thee, to love one. If he be base, thy blood will make him noble; if beggarly, thy goods shall make him wealthy; if a stranger, thy freedom may enfranchise him; if he be young, he is the more fitter to be thy fere; if he be old, the liker to thine aged father. For I had rather thou shouldst lead a life to thine own liking in earth, than to thy great torments lead apes in Hell. Be bold, therefore, to make me partner of thy desire, which will be partaker of thy disease, yea, and a furtherer of thy delights, as far as either my friends or my lands or my life will stretch.'

Lucilla, perceiving the drift of the old fox her father, weighed with herself what was best to be done. At the last, not weighing her father's ill-will, but encouraged by love, shaped him an answer which pleased Ferardo but a little and pinched Philautus on the parson's side[189] on this manner:

'Dear father Ferardo, although I see the bait you lay to catch me, yet I am content to swallow the hook; neither are you more desirous to take me napping, than I willing to confess my meaning. So it is that love hath as well inveigled me as others which make it as strange as I.[190] Neither do I love him so meanly that I should be ashamed of his name, neither is his personage so mean

---

[189] *pinched . . . side*] proverbial. To rob the parson of his tithes (i.e. deprive Philautus of his chance to marry).   [190] *make it as strange as I*] repudiate it as much as I have

that I should love him shamefully. It is Euphues that lately arrived here at Naples that hath battered the bulwark of my breast and shall shortly enter as conqueror into my bosom. What his wealth is, I neither know it nor weigh it; what his wit is, all Naples doth know it and wonder at it; neither have I been curious to enquire of his progenitors, for that I know so noble a mind could take no original but from a noble man: for as no bird can look again[191] the sun but those that be bred of the eagle, neither any hawk soar so high as the brood of the hobby,[192] so no wight can have such excellent qualities except he descend of a noble race, neither be of so high capacity unless he issue of a high progeny. And I hope Philautus will not be my foe, seeing I have chosen his dear friend, neither you, father, be displeased in that Philautus is displaced. You need not muse that I should so suddenly be entangled; love gives no reason of choice, neither will it suffer any repulse. Myrrha was enamoured of her natural father, Biblis of her brother, Phaedra of her son-in-law.[193] If nature can no way resist the fury of affection, how should it be stayed by wisdom?'

Ferardo, interrupting her in the middle of her discourse, although he were moved with inward grudge, yet he wisely repressed his anger, knowing that sharp words would but sharpen her froward will, and thus answered her briefly:

'Lucilla, as I am not presently to grant my good will, so mean I not to reprehend thy choice. Yet wisdom willeth me to pause until I have called what may happen to my remembrance, and warneth thee to be circumspect lest thy rash conceit bring a sharp repentance. As for you, Philautus, I would not have you despair, seeing a woman doth oftentimes change her desire.'

Unto whom Philautus in few words made answer: 'Certainly, Ferardo, I take the less grief in that I see her so greedy after Euphues; and by so much the more I am content to leave my suit, by how much the more she seemeth to disdain my service. But as for hope, because I would not by any means taste one dram thereof, I will abjure all places of her abode and loathe her company,

---

[191] *again*] against, i.e. into   [192] *hobby*] small member of the falcon family
[193] *Myrrha / Biblis / Phaedra*] all examples of unnatural love, probably drawn from Ovid

whose countenance I have so much loved. As for Euphues –.'
And there staying his speech, he flung out of the doors and,
repairing to his lodging, uttered these words:

'Ah most dissembling wretch Euphues! O counterfeit companion! Couldst thou under the show of a steadfast friend cloak the
malice of a mortal foe; under the colour of simplicity shroud the
image of deceit? Is thy Livia turned to my Lucilla, thy love to my
lover, thy devotion to my saint? Is this the courtesy of Athens, the
cavilling of scholars, the craft of Grecians? Couldst thou not
remember, Philautus, that Greece is never without some wily
Ulysses, never void of some Sinon,[194] never to seek of some
deceitful shifter? Is it not commonly said of Grecians that craft
cometh to them by kind, that they learn to deceive in their cradle?
Why then did his pretended courtesy bewitch thee with such
credulity? Shall my good will be the cause of his ill will? Because
I was content to be his friend, thought he me meet to be made his
fool? I see now that as the fish Scolopidus in the flood Araris at
the waxing of the moon is as white as the driven snow, and at the
waning as black as the burnt coal,[195] so Euphues, which at the
first increasing of our familiarity was very zealous, is now at the
last cast become most faithless.

'But why rather exclaim I not against Lucilla, whose wanton
looks caused Euphues to violate his plighted faith? Ah wretched
wench, canst thou be so light of love as to change with every
wind, so unconstant as to prefer a new lover before thine old
friend? Ah, well I wot that a new broom sweepeth clean, and a
new garment maketh thee leave off the old though it be fitter, and
new wine causeth thee to forsake the old though it be better;
much like to the men in the island Scyrum which pull up the
old tree when they see the young begin to spring, and not unlike
unto the widow of Lesbos[196] which changed all her old gold for

---

[194] *Ulysses / Sinon*] examples of Greek cunning. Ulysses, renowned for his
shrewdness, proposed the stratagem of the wooden horse that brought about the
fall of Troy. Sinon persuaded the Trojans to draw the horse into their city.
[195] *the fish Scolopidus . . . burnt coal*] one of several mythological creatures said to
change size or colour with the changing of the moon   [196] *Scyrum . . . Lesbos*]
islands in the Aegean sea. The source of the comparisons is unknown.

new glass. Have I served thee three years faithfully, and am I served so unkindly? Shall the fruit of my desire be turned to disdain?

'But unless Euphues had inveigled thee thou hadst yet been constant; yea, but if Euphues had not seen thee willing to be won he would never have wooed thee. But had not Euphues enticed thee with fair words thou wouldst never have loved him; but hadst thou not given him fair looks he would never have liked thee. Aye, but Euphues gave the onset; aye, but Lucilla gave the occasion. Aye, but Euphues first brake his mind;[197] aye, but Lucilla first bewrayed her meaning. Tush, why go I about to excuse any of them, seeing I have just cause to accuse them both? Neither ought I to dispute which of them hath proffered me the greatest villainy, sith that either of them hath committed perjury. Yet although they have found me dull in perceiving their falsehood, they shall not find me slack in revenging their folly. As for Lucilla, seeing I mean altogether to forget her, I mean also to forgive her, lest in seeking means to be revenged, mine old desire be renewed.'

Philautus, having thus discoursed with himself, began to write to Euphues as followeth:

'Although hitherto, Euphues, I have shrined thee in my heart for a trusty friend, I will shun thee hereafter as a trothless foe; and although I cannot see in thee less wit than I was wont, yet do I find less honesty. I perceive at the last (although, being deceived, it be too late) that musk, although it be sweet in the smell, is sour in the smack;[198] that the leaf of the cedar tree, though it be fair to be seen, yet the syrup depriveth sight; that friendship, though it be plighted by shaking the hand, yet it is shaken off by fraud of the heart.

'But thou hast not much to boast of, for as thou hast won a fickle lady so hast thou lost a faithful friend. How canst thou be secure of her constancy, when thou hast had such trial of her lightness; how canst thou assure thyself that she will be faithful to thee, which hath been faithless to me?

'Ah Euphues, let not my credulity be an occasion hereafter for

---

[197] *brake his mind*] revealed his thoughts   [198] *smack*] taste

thee to practise the like cruelty. Remember this, that yet there hath never been any faithless to his friend that hath not also been fruitless to his God. But I weigh this treachery the less in that it cometh from a Grecian in whom is no troth. Though I be too weak to wrestle for a revenge, yet God, who permitteth no guile to be guiltless, will shortly requite this injury; though Philautus have no policy to undermine thee, yet thine own practices will be sufficient to overthrow thee.

'Couldst thou, Euphues, for the love of a fruitless pleasure violate the league of faithful friendship; didst thou weigh more the enticing looks of a lewd wench than the entire love of a loyal friend? If thou didst determine with thyself at the first to be false, why didst thou swear to be true; if to be true, why art thou false? If thou wast minded both falsely and forgedly to deceive me, why didst thou flatter and dissemble with me at the first; if to love me, why didst thou flinch at the last? If the sacred bands of amity did delight thee, why didst thou break them; if dislike thee, why didst thou praise them? Dost thou not know that a perfect friend should be like the glaze-worm[199] which shineth most bright in the dark; or like the pure frankincense which smelleth most sweet when it is in the fire; or, at the least, not unlike to the damask rose which is sweeter in the still than on the stalk? But thou, Euphues, dost rather resemble the swallow which in the summer creepeth under the eaves of every house and in the winter leaveth nothing but dirt behind her; or the humble-bee which having sucked honey out of the fair flower doth leave it and loathe it; or the spider which in the finest web doth hang the fairest fly.

'Dost thou think, Euphues, that thy craft in betraying me shall any whit cool my courage in revenging thy villainy or that a gentleman of Naples will put up such an injury at the hands of a scholar? And if I do, it is not for want of strength to maintain my just quarrel, but of will which thinketh scorn to get so vain a conquest. I know that Menelaus for his ten years' war endured ten years' woe, that after all his strife he won but a strumpet, that for all his travails he reduced[200] (I cannot say reclaimed) but a

---

[199] *glaze-worm*] glow-worm   [200] *reduced*] brought back

straggler; which was as much, in my judgement, as to strive for a broken glass which is good for nothing. I wish thee rather Menelaus' care than myself his conquest; that thou, being deluded by Lucilla, mayest rather know what it is to be deceived, than I, having conquered thee, should prove what it were to bring back a dissembler. Seeing, therefore, there can no greater revenge light upon thee than that, as thou hast reaped where another hath sown, so another may thresh that which thou hast reaped, I will pray that thou mayest be measured unto with the like measure that thou hast meten[201] unto others; that as thou hast thought it no conscience to betray me, so others may deem it no dishonesty to deceive thee; that as Lucilla made it a light matter to forswear her old friend Philautus, so she may make it a mock to forsake her new fere Euphues. Which if it come to pass, as it is like by my compass, then shalt thou see the troubles and feel the torments which thou hast already thrown into the hearts and eyes of others. Thus hoping shortly to see thee as hopeless as myself is hapless, I wish my wish were as effectually ended as it is heartily looked for. And so I leave thee.

Thine once,
Philautus'

Philautus, dispatching a messenger with this letter speedily to Euphues, went into the fields to walk there, either to digest his choler or chew upon his melancholy. But Euphues having read the contents was well content, setting his talk at naught and answering his taunts in these gibing terms:

'I remember Philautus how valiantly Ajax boasted in the feats of arms, yet Ulysses bare away the armour;[202] and it may be that though thou crack[203] of thine own courage, thou mayest easily lose the conquest. Dost thou think Euphues such a dastard that he is not able to withstand thy courage, or such a dullard that he cannot descry[204] thy craft. Alas, good soul! It fareth with thee as with the hen which, when the puttock[205] hath caught her chicken,

---

[201] *meten*] meted, i.e. measured out   [202] *Ajax . . . armour*] A reference to the contest between Ajax and Ulysses for the armour of Achilles, won by Ulysses because of his superior eloquence in recounting his deeds.
[203] *crack*] boast   [204] *descry*] perceive   [205] *puttock*] kite

beginneth to cackle; and thou, having lost thy lover, beginnest to prattle.

'Tush, Philautus, I am in this point of Euripedes his mind,[206] who thinks it lawful, for the desire of a kingdom, to transgress the bounds of honesty, and, for the love of a lady, to violate and break the bands of amity. The friendship between man and man as it is common so is it of course, between man and woman as it is seldom so is it sincere; the one proceedeth of the similitude of manners, the other of the sincerity of the heart. If thou hadst learned the first point of hawking, thou wouldst have learned to have held fast; or the first note of descant, thou wouldst have kept thy *sol fa* to thyself.[207]

'But thou canst blame me no more of folly in leaving thee to love Lucilla than thou mayest reprove him of foolishness that having a sparrow in his hand letteth her go to catch the pheasant, or him of unskilfulness that seeing the heron leaveth to level his shot at the stock-dove, or that woman of coyness that having a dead rose in her bosom throweth it away to gather the fresh violet. Love knoweth no laws. Did not Jupiter transform himself into the shape of Amphitryon to embrace Alcmene; into the form of a swan to enjoy Leda; into a bull to beguile Io; into a shower of gold to win Danae? Did not Neptune change himself into a heifer, a ram, a flood, a dolphin, only for the love of those he lusted after? Did not Apollo convert himself into a shepherd, into a bird, into a lion, for the desire he had to heal his disease? If the gods thought no scorn to become beasts to obtain their best beloved, shall Euphues be so nice in changing his copy to gain his lady? No, no; he that cannot dissemble in love is not worthy to live. I am of this mind, that both might and malice, deceit and treachery, all perjury, any impiety may lawfully be committed in love, which is lawless.

'In that thou arguest Lucilla of lightness, thy will hangs in the light of thy wit.[208] Dost thou not know that the weak stomach, if

---

[206] *Euripedes his mind*] Source of reference unknown [207] *first note of descant . . . thyself*] image drawn from singing in consort. If you keep your part to yourself others cannot join in. [208] *thy will . . . thy wit*] your desires are obscuring your judgement

it be cloyed with one diet, doth soon surfeit; that the clown's[209] garlic cannot ease the courtier's disease so well as the pure treacle; that far fet and dear bought is good for ladies;[210] that Euphues being a more dainty morsel than Philautus ought better to be accepted?

'Tush, Philautus, set thy heart at rest, for thy hap willeth thee to give over all hope both of my friendship and her love. As for revenge, thou are not so able to lend a blow as I to ward it, neither more venturous to challenge the combat than I valiant to answer the quarrel. As Lucilla was caught by fraud so shall she be kept by force, and as thou wast too simple to espy my craft so I think thou wilt be too weak to withstand my courage; but if thy revenge stand only upon thy wish, thou shalt never live to see my woe or to have thy will. And so farewell.

Euphues.'

This letter being dispatched, Euphues sent it and Philautus read it; who, disdaining those proud terms, disdained also to answer them, being ready to ride with Ferardo.

Euphues, having for a space absented himself from the house of Ferardo because he was at home, longed sore to see Lucilla, which now opportunity offered unto him, Ferardo being gone again to Venice with Philautus. But in his absence one Curio, a gentleman of Naples of little wealth and less wit, haunted Lucilla her company, and so enchanted her that Euphues was also cast off with Philautus; which thing being unknown to Euphues caused him the sooner to make his repair to the presence of his lady, whom he finding in her muses began pleasantly to salute in this manner:

'Mistress Lucilla, although my long absence might breed your just anger (for that lovers desire nothing so much as often meeting), yet I hope my presence will dissolve your choler (for that lovers are soon pleased when of their wishes they be fully possessed). My absence is the rather to be excused in that your father hath been always at home, whose frowns seemed to threaten my

---

[209] *clown's*] rustic's   [210] *far fet [i.e. fetched] and dear bought is good for ladies*] proverbial. Women like unusual things that are not cheaply obtained.

ill fortune, and my presence at this present the better to be accepted in that I have made such speedy repair to your presence.'

Unto whom Lucilla answered with this gleek:[211] 'Truly, Euphues, you have missed the cushion,[212] for I was neither angry with your long absence, neither am I well pleased at your presence; the one gave me rather a good hope hereafter never to see you, the other giveth me a greater occasion to abhor you.'

Euphues, being nipped on the head,[213] with a pale countenance, as though his soul had forsaken his body, replied as followeth: 'If this sudden change, Lucilla, proceed of any desert of mine, I am here not only to answer the fact, but also to make amends for my fault; if of any new motion or mind to forsake your new friend, I am rather to lament your inconstancy than revenge it. But I hope that such hot love cannot be so soon cold, neither such sure faith be rewarded with so sudden forgetfulness.'

Lucilla, not ashamed to confess her folly, answered him with this frump:[214] 'Sir, whether your deserts or my desire have wrought his change it will boot you little to know; neither do I crave amends, neither fear revenge. As for fervent love, you know there is no fire so hot but it is quenched with water, neither affection so strong but is weakened with reason. Let this suffice thee, that thou know I care not for thee.'

'Indeed,' said Euphues, 'to know the cause of your alteration would boot me little, seeing the effect taketh such force. I have heard that women either love entirely or hate deadly, and seeing you have put me out of doubt of the one, I must needs persuade myself of the other. This change will cause Philautus to laugh me to scorn, and double thy lightness in turning so often. Such was the hope that I conceived of thy constancy that I spared not in all places to blaze[215] thy loyalty, but now my rash conceit will prove me a liar and thee a light huswife.'

'Nay,' said Lucilla, 'now shalt not thou laugh Philautus to scorn, seeing you have both drunk of one cup. In misery, Euphues, it is a great comfort to have a companion. I doubt not but that you .will both conspire against me to work some mischief, although I

---

[211] *gleek*] jibe [212] *have missed the cushion*] are mistaken [213] *nipped on the head*] painfully checked [214] *frump*] jibe [215] *blaze*] proclaim

nothing fear your malice. Whosoever accounteth you a liar for praising me, may also deem you a lecher for being enamoured of me; and whosoever judgeth me light in forsaking of you, may think thee as lewd in loving of me; for thou that thoughtest it lawful to deceive thy friend, must take no scorn to be deceived of thy foe.'

'Then I perceive, Lucilla,' said he, 'that I was made thy stale, and Philautus thy laughing-stock; whose friendship (I must confess indeed) I have refused, to obtain thy favour. And sithence another hath won that we both have lost, I am content for my part; neither ought I to be grieved seeing thou art fickle.'

'Certes, Euphues,' said Lucilla, 'you spend your wind in waste, for your welcome is but small and your cheer is like to be less. Fancy giveth no reason of his change, neither will be controlled for any choice. This is, therefore, to warn you that from henceforth you neither solicit this suit, neither offer any way your service. I have chosen one, I must needs confess, neither to be compared to Philautus in wealth, nor to thee in wit, neither in birth to the worst of you both. I think God gave it me for a just plague for renouncing Philautus and choosing thee; and sithence I am an example to all women of lightness, I am like also to be a mirror to them all of unhappiness; which ill luck I must take by so much the more patiently, by how much the more I acknowledge myself to have deserved it worthily.'

'Well, Lucilla,' answered Euphues, 'this case breedeth my sorrow the more in that it is so sudden, and by so much the more I lament it, by how much the less I looked for it. In that my welcome is so cold and my cheer so simple, it nothing toucheth me (seeing your fury is so hot and my misfortune so great) that I am neither willing to receive it nor you to bestow it. If tract of time or want of trial had caused this metamorphosis, my grief had been more tolerable and your fleeting more excusable; but coming in a moment undeserved, unlooked for, unthought of, it increaseth my sorrow and thy shame.'

'Euphues,' quoth she, 'you make a long harvest for a little corn, and angle for the fish that is already caught. Curio, yea Curio, is he that hath my love at his pleasure, and shall also have my life at his commandment; and although you deem him unworthy to

58

enjoy that which erst you accounted no wight worthy to embrace, yet seeing I esteem him more worth than any, he is to be reputed as chief. The wolf chooseth him for her make[216] that hath or doth endure most travail for her sake; Venus was content to take the blacksmith with his polt-foot;[217] Cornelia here in Naples disdained not to love a rude miller.[218] As for changing, did not Helen, the pearl of Greece, thy countrywoman, first take Menelaus, then Theseus, and last of all Paris? If brute beasts give us examples that those are most to be liked of whom we are best beloved, or if the princess of beauty, Venus, and her heirs, Helen and Cornelia, show that our affection standeth on our free will, then am I rather to be excused than accused. Therefore, good Euphues, be as merry as you may be, for time may so turn that once again you may be.'

'Nay, Lucilla,' said he, 'my harvest shall cease, seeing others have reaped my corn; as for angling for the fish that is already caught, that were but mere folly. But in my mind, if you be a fish, you are either an eel which as soon as one hath hold of her tail will slip out of his hand, or else a minnow which will be nibbling at every bait but never biting. But what fish soever you be, you have made both me and Philautus to swallow a gudgeon.

'If Curio be the person, I would neither wish thee a greater plague, nor him a deadlier poison. I, for my part, think him worthy of thee, and thou unworthy of him: for, although he be in body deformed, in mind foolish, an innocent born, a beggar by misfortune, yet doth he deserve a better than thyself, whose corrupt manners have stained thy heavenly hue, whose light behaviour hath dimmed the lights of thy beauty, whose unconstant mind hath betrayed the innocency of so many a gentleman.

'And in that you bring in the example of a beast to confirm your folly you show therein your beastly disposition, which is ready to follow such beastliness. But Venus played false – and what for that? Seeing her lightness serveth for an example, I would wish thou mightest try her punishment for a reward, that

216 *make*] mate   217 *blacksmith . . . polt-foot*] Vulcan (Roman god of fire), who was born with a club foot   218 *Cornelia . . . miller*] A reference to the type of story that occurs in Boccaccio's *Decameron*, but the tale itself is unknown.

being openly taken in an iron net all the world might judge whether thou be fish or flesh – and certes, in my mind no angle[219] will hold thee, it must be a net. Cornelia loved a miller, and thou a miser: can her folly excuse thy fault? Helen of Greece, my countrywoman born but thine by profession, changed and rechanged at her pleasure, I grant: shall the lewdness of others animate thee in thy lightness? Why then dost thou not haunt the stews because Lais[220] frequented them; why dost thou not love a bull seeing Pasiphae[221] loved one; why art thou not enamoured of thy father knowing that Myrrha was so incensed? These are set down that we, viewing their incontinency, should fly the like impudency, not follow the like excess; neither can they excuse thee of any inconstancy.

'Merry I will be as I may; but if I may hereafter as thou meanest, I will not. And therefore farewell Lucilla, the most inconstant that ever was nursed in Naples; farewell Naples, the most cursed town in all Italy; and women all, farewell.'

Euphues, having thus given her his last farewell, yet, being solitary, began afresh to recount his sorrow on this manner:

'Ah Euphues, into what a quandary art thou brought! In what sudden misfortune art thou wrapped! It is like to fare with thee as with the eagle, which dieth neither for age nor with sickness, but with famine;[222] for although thy stomach hunger, yet thy heart will not suffer thee to eat. And why shouldst thou torment thyself for one in whom is neither faith nor fervency? Oh the counterfeit love of women! Oh inconstant sex! I have lost Philautus; I have lost Lucilla; I have lost that which I shall hardly find again, a faithful friend.

'Ah foolish Euphues, why didst thou leave Athens, the nurse of wisdom, to inhabit Naples, the nourisher of wantonness? Had it not been better for thee to have eaten salt with the philosophers

---

[219] *angle*] fish hook. The reference is to the public humiliation of Venus by her husband (Vulcan) who caught her with her lover (Mars) in an invisible net and exposed her to the mirth of the gods.   [220] *Lais*] a celebrated Corinthian courtesan   [221] *Pasiphae*] wife of King Minos and mother, by a bull, of the minotaur, a monster with a human body and bull's head   [222] *eagle . . . famine*] eagles were reputed to die from hunger because their beaks grew too long to allow them to eat.

in Greece than sugar with the courtiers of Italy? But behold the course of youth which always inclineth to pleasure. I forsook mine old companions to search for new friends; I rejected the grave and fatherly counsel of Eubulus to follow the brainsick humour of mine own will. I addicted myself wholly to the service of women, to spend my life in the laps of ladies, my lands in maintenance of bravery, my wit in the vanities of idle sonnets. I had thought that women had been as we men, that is, true, faithful, zealous, constant; but I perceive they be rather woe unto men by their falsehood, jealousy, inconstancy. I was half persuaded that they were made of the perfection of men, and would be comforters, but now I see they have tasted of the infection of the serpent, and will be corrosives. The physician saith it is dangerous to minister physic unto the patient that hath a cold stomach and a hot liver, lest in giving warmth to the one he inflame the other; so verily it is hard to deal with a woman whose words seem fervent, whose heart is congealed into hard ice, lest trusting their outward talk, he be betrayed with their inward treachery.

'I will to Athens there to toss my books, no more in Naples to live with fair looks. I will so frame myself as all youth hereafter shall rather rejoice to see mine amendment, than be animated to follow my former life. Philosophy, physic, divinity shall be my study. Oh the hidden secrets of nature, the express image of moral virtues, the equal balance of justice, the medicines to heal all diseases, how they begin to delight me! The axioms of Aristotle, the maxims of Justinian, the aphorisms of Galen[223] have suddenly made such a breach into my mind that I seem only to desire them, which did only erst detest them.

'If wit be employed in the honest study of learning, what thing so precious as wit; if in the idle trade of love, what thing more pestilent than wit? The proof of late hath been verified in me, whom nature hath endued with a little wit which I have abused with an obstinate will. Most true it is that the thing the better it is the greater is the abuse: and that there is nothing but through the malice of man may be abused. Doth not the fire (an element so necessary that without it man cannot live) as well burn the

[223]   *axioms of Aristotle . . . Galen*] tenets of philosophy, law and medicine

house as burn in the house, if it be abused; doth not treacle as well poison as help if it be taken out of time; doth not wine if it be immoderately taken kill the stomach, enflame the liver, murder the drunken; doth not physic destroy if it be not well tempered; doth not law accuse if it be not rightly interpreted; doth not divinity condemn if it be not faithfully construed? Is not poison taken out of the honeysuckle by the spider, venom out of the rose by the canker, dung out of the maple tree by the scorpion? Even so the greatest wickedness is drawn out of the greatest wit if it be abused by will, or entangled with the world, or inveigled with women.

'But seeing I see mine own impiety, I will endeavour myself to amend all that is past, and to be a mirror of godliness hereafter. The rose, though a little it be eaten with the canker, yet being distilled yieldeth sweet water; the iron, though fretted with the rust, yet being burnt in the fire shineth brighter; and wit, although it hath been eaten with the canker of his own conceit and fretted with the rust of vain love, yet being purified in the still of wisdom and tried in the fire of zeal, will shine bright and smell sweet in the nostrils of all young novices.

'As, therefore, I gave a farewell to Lucilla, a farewell to Naples, a farewell to women, so now do I give a farewell to the world, meaning rather to macerate[224] myself with melancholy than pine in folly, rather choosing to die in my study amidst my books than to court it in Italy in the company of ladies.'

It happened immediately Ferardo to return home, who hearing this strange event, was not a little amazed, and was now more ready to exhort Lucilla from the love of Curio, than before to the liking of Philautus. Therefore, in all haste, with watery eyes and a woeful heart, began on this manner to reason with his daughter:

'Lucilla (daughter I am ashamed to call thee, seeing thou hast neither care of thy father's tender affection, nor of thine own credit), what sprite hath enchanted thy spirit that every minute thou alterest thy mind? I had thought that my hoary hairs should have found comfort by thy golden locks, and my rotten age great

---

[224]   *macerate*] waste away

ease by thy ripe years. But alas, I see in thee neither wit to order thy doings, neither will to frame thyself to discretion, neither the nature of a child, neither the nurture of a maiden, neither (I cannot without tears speak it) any regard of thine honour, neither any care of thine honesty. I am now enforced to remember thy mother's death, who I think was a prophetess in her life; for oftentimes she would say that thou hadst more beauty than was convenient for one that should be honest, and more cockering than was meet for one that should be a matron.

'Would I had never lived to be so old, or thou to be so obstinate; either would I had died in my youth in the court, or thou in thy cradle; I would to God that either I had never been born, or thou never bred. Is this the comfort that the parent reapeth for all his care? Is obstinacy paid for obedience, stubbornness rendered for duty, malicious desperateness for filial fear? I perceive now that the wise painter saw more than the foolish parent can, who painted love going downward, saying it might well descend but ascend it could never. Danaus, whom they report to be the father of fifty children, had among them all but one that disobeyed him in a thing most dishonest; [225] but I that am father to one more than I would be, although one be all, have that one most disobedient to me in a request lawful and reasonable. If Danaus seeing but one of his daughters without awe became himself without mercy, what shall Ferardo do in this case who hath one and all most unnatural to him in a most just cause?

'Shall Curio enjoy the fruit of my travails, possess the benefit of my labours, inherit the patrimony of mine ancestors, who hath neither wisdom to increase them, nor wit to keep them? Wilt thou, Lucilla, bestow thyself on such an one as hath neither comeliness in his body, nor knowledge in his mind, nor credit in his country? Oh I would thou hadst either been ever faithful to Philautus, or never faithless to Euphues, or would thou wouldst be more fickle to Curio. As thy beauty hath made thee the blaze of Italy, so will thy lightness make thee the byword of the world. O Lucilla, Lucilla, would thou wert less fair or more fortunate,

---

[225] *Danaus . . . dishonest*] father of fifty daughters, all of whom, except Hypermnestra, murdered their husbands at his command

either of less honour or greater honesty, either better minded or soon buried!

'Shall thine old father live to see thee match with a young fool; shall my kind heart be rewarded with such unkind hate? Ah Lucilla, thou knowest not the care of a father, nor the duty of a child; and as far art thou from piety as I from cruelty. Nature will not permit me to disherit my daughter, and yet it will suffer thee to dishonour thy father. Affection causeth me to wish thy life, and shall it entice thee to procure my death? It is mine only comfort to see thee flourish in thy youth, and is it thine to see me fade in mine age? To conclude, I desire to live to see thee prosper, and thou to see me perish.

'But why cast I the effect of this unnaturalness in thy teeth, seeing I myself was the cause? I made thee a wanton, and thou hast made me a fool; I brought thee up like a cockney and thou hast handled me like a coxcomb[226] (I speak it to mine own shame); I made more of thee than became a father, and thou less of me than beseemed a child. And shall my loving care be cause of thy wicked cruelty? Yea, yea, I am not the first that hath been too careful, nor the last that shall be handled so unkindly; it is common to see fathers too fond, and children too froward.

'Well Lucilla, the tears which thou seest trickle down my cheeks and the drops of blood (which thou canst not see) that fall from my heart enforce me to make an end of my talk. And if thou have any duty of a child, or care of a friend, or courtesy of a stranger, or feeling of a Christian, or humanity of a reasonable creature, then release thy father of grief and acquit thyself of ungratefulness. Otherwise thou shalt but hasten my death, and increase thine own defame; which if thou do, the gain is mine, and the loss thine, and both infinite.'

Lucilla, either so bewitched that she could not relent, or so wicked that she would not yield to her father's request, answered him on this manner:

'Dear father, as you would have me to show the duty of a child, so ought you to show the care of a parent; and as the one standeth in obedience so the other is grounded upon reason. You would

226   *cockney / coxcomb*] over-indulged child / fool

have me, as I owe duty to you, to leave Curio; and I desire you, as you owe me any love, that you suffer me to enjoy him. If you accuse me of unnaturalness in that I yield not to your request, I am also to condemn you of unkindness in that you grant not my petition. You object I know not what to Curio; but it is the eye of the master that fatteth the horse,[227] and the love of the woman that maketh the man. To give reason for fancy were to weigh the fire and measure the wind. If, therefore, my delight be the cause of your death, I think my sorrow would be an occasion of your solace. And if you be angry because I am pleased, certes I deem you would be content if I were deceased; which if it be so that my pleasure breed your pain and mine annoy your joy, I may well say that you are an unkind father and I an unfortunate child. But, good father, either content yourself with my choice, or let me stand to the main chance;[228] otherwise the grief will be mine, and the fault yours, and both untolerable.'

Ferardo, seeing his daughter to have neither regard of her own honour nor his request, conceived such an inward grief that in short space he died, leaving Lucilla the only heir of his lands and Curio to possess them. But what end came of her, seeing it is nothing incident to the history of Euphues, it were superfluous to insert it, and so incredible that all women would rather wonder at it than believe it. Which event being so strange, I had rather leave them in a muse what it should be than in a maze in telling what it was.

Philautus, having intelligence of Euphues his success and the falsehood of Lucilla, although he began to rejoice at the misery of his fellow, yet seeing her fickleness, could not but lament her folly and pity his friend's misfortune, thinking that the lightness of Lucilla enticed Euphues to so great liking. Euphues and Philautus having conference between themselves, casting discourtesy in the teeth each of the other, but chiefly noting disloyalty in the demeanour of Lucilla, after much talk renewed their old friendship, both abandoning Lucilla as most abominable. Philautus was

---

[227]   *the eye of the master fatteth the horse*] proverbial, cf. beauty is in the eye of the beholder   [228]   *stand to the main chance*] gambling term. Abide by my major venture.

earnest to have Euphues tarry in Naples, and Euphues desirous to have Philautus to Athens; but the one was so addicted to the court, the other so wedded to the university, that each refused the offer of the other. Yet this they agreed between themselves, that though their bodies were by distance of place severed, yet the conjunction of their minds should neither be separated by the length of time, nor alienated by change of soil. 'I, for my part,' said Euphues, 'to confirm this league give thee my hand and my heart.' And so likewise did Philautus.

And so, shaking hands, they bid each other farewell.

CAMPASPE

[Dramatis Personae

Alexander, *King of Macedon*
Hephestion, *his general*
Clitus } *Macedonian officers*
Parmenio
Campaspe } *Theban captives*
Timoclea
Melippus, *a courtier*
Plato
Aristotle
Cleanthes
Anaxarchus } *philosophers*
Crates
Chrysippus
Diogenes
Crysus, *a Cynic Beggar*

Apelles, *a painter*
Manes, *servant to Diogenes*
Granichus, *servant to Plato*
Psyllus, *servant to Apelles*
Solinus, *a citizen of Athens*
Sylvius, *another citizen*
Perim
Milo } *his sons*
Trico
Lais, *a courtesan*
Milectus } *soldiers, her customers*
Phrygius
Populus
Page, *to Alexander*
Captives

Scene: *Athens*]

68

The Prologue at the Blackfriars

They that fear the stinging of wasps make fans of peacocks' tails, whose spots are like eyes; and Lepidus, which could not sleep for the chatting of birds, set up a beast whose head was like a dragon; and we which stand in awe of report are compelled to set before our owl Pallas' shield, thinking by her 5 virtue to cover the other's deformity. It was a sign of famine to Egypt when Nilus flowed less than twelve cubits or more than eighteen, and it may threaten despair unto us if we be less curious than you look for or more cumbersome. But as Theseus, being promised to be brought to an eagle's nest, 10 and travelling all the day found but a wren in a hedge, yet said, 'This is a bird', so we hope, if the shower of our swelling mountain seem to bring forth some elephant, perform but a mouse, you will gently say, 'This is a beast'. Basil softly touched yieldeth a sweet scent, but chafed in the hand a rank 15 savour. We fear even so that our labours, slyly glanced on, will breed some content, but examined to the proof, small commendation. The haste in performing shall be our excuse. There went two nights to the begetting of Hercules, feathers appear not on the phoenix under seven months, and the mul- 20 berry is twelve in budding; but our travails are like the hare's who at one time bringeth forth, nourisheth and engendreth again, or like the brood of trochilus, whose eggs in the same moment that they are laid become birds. But howsoever we

---

2-4 *Lepidus . . . dragon*] The picture of a large snake was reputedly used to silence birds disturbing the sleep of Lepidus, a member of the Roman triumvirate (died 13 BC). 5 *owl*] nocturnal bird thought unfit to be seen by day, and hence associated with monstrosity 5 *Pallas' shield*] impregnable defence (The shield bore the head of the Medusa which turned all who looked on it to stone.) 10-12 *Theseus . . . bird*] The legendary hero of Atticus who went in search of the golden fleece. No source is known for the tale of the eagle and the wren. 19 *There went . . . Hercules*] Jupiter, having substituted himself for the husband of Alcmena, caused the night to be unnaturally prolonged while he was with her during which time Hercules was conceived. 20 *phoenix*] fabulous bird of extreme longevity (hence its slowness to fledge) 20-1 *mulberry . . . budding*] recorded by Pliny 23 *brood of trochilus*] See above p.13n. The story about the eggs appears to be Lyly's invention.

finish our work, we crave pardon if we offend in matter, and 25
patience if we transgress in manners. We have mixed mirth
with counsel and discipline with delight, thinking it not amiss
in the same garden to sow pot-herbs that we set flowers. But
we hope, as harts that cast their horns, snakes their skins,
eagles their bills, become more fresh for any other labour, so 30
our charge being shaken off, we shall be fit for greater matters. But lest, like the Myndians, we make our gates greater
than our town, and that our play runs out at the preface, we
here conclude, wishing that although there be in your precise
judgements an universal mislike, yet we may enjoy by your 35
wonted courtesies a general silence.

27 *discipline*] instruction   28 *pot-herbs*] herbs grown for culinary purposes
30 *eagles their bills*] for the renewal of the eagle, see *Gallathea*, III.iv.38n. below

The Prologue at the Court

We are ashamed that our bird, which fluttered by twilight seeming a swan, should be proved a bat set against the sun. But as Jupiter placed Silenus' ass among the stars, and Alcibiades covered his pictures, being owls and apes, with a curtain embroidered with lions and eagles, so are we 5 enforced upon a rough discourse to draw on a smooth excuse, resembling lapidaries, who think to hide the crack in a stone by setting it deep in gold. The gods supped once with poor Baucis; the Persian kings sometimes shaved sticks; our hope is your Highness will at this time lend an ear to an idle 10 pastime. Appion, raising Homer from hell, demanded only who was his father; and we, calling Alexander from his grave, seek only who was his love. Whatsoever we present, we wish it may be thought the dancing of Agrippa his shadows, who, in the moment they were seen, were of any shape one would 15 conceive; or lynxes, who, having a quick sight to discern, have a short memory to forget. With us it is like to fare as with these torches which, giving light to others, consume themselves; and we, showing delight to others, shame ourselves. 20

1-2 *We are ashamed . . . sun*] A reference to the two venues at which the play was performed: the Blackfriars, where it was successful, and the Court (i.e. before the Queen) where any deficiencies would be perceived. 3 *Jupiter . . . stars*] The ass which carried the satyr, Silenus, was thought to have been set among the stars for the help he afforded Jupiter in his battle against the giants. (See Hunter (ed.), *Campaspe*, p.52n and *Gallathea*, III.iv.48n below.) 4 *Alcibiades*] Athenian statesman and military leader (450-404 BC). No source is known for the allusion to his pictures. 7 *lapidaries*] workers with precious stones 9 *Baucis*] wife of Philemon. The aged couple gave hospitality to the disguised Jupiter when their richer neighbours declined to receive him. 9 *shaved sticks*] whittled wood (as a means of passing the time on a journey) 11 *Appion*] Greek grammarian and student of Homer, thought to have raised the spirit of the poet in order to confirm details of his biography. 14 *Agrippa*] Henry Cornelius Agrippa (1486-1535), humanist scholar and magician, noted for the 'shadows' he could conjure up. (See Hunter (ed.) *Campaspe*, p.53n to which I am indebted.) 18 *these torches*] i.e. the wax lights illuminating the room in which the play was staged (cf. The Epilogue at the Court p.129 below).

Actus Primus

[*Enter*] CLITUS [*and*] PARMENIO.

Clitus. Parmenio, I cannot tell whether I should more commend in Alexander's victories courage or courtesy, in the
one being a resolution without fear, in the other a liberali-
ty above custom: Thebes is razed, the people not racked;
towers thrown down, bodies not thrust aside; a conquest   5
without conflict, and a cruel war in a mild peace.

Parmenio. Clitus, it becometh the son of Philip to be none
other than Alexander is; therefore, seeing in the father a
full perfection, who could have doubted in the son an
an excellency? For as the moon can borrow nothing else of   10
the sun but light, so of a sire in whom nothing but virtue
was, what could the child receive but singular? It is for
turquoise to stain each other, not for diamonds; in the one
to be made a difference in goodness, in the other no comparison.   15

Clitus. You mistake me, Parmenio, if, whilst I commend
Alexander, you imagine I call Philip into question – unless
happily you conjecture (which none of judgement will
conceive) that because I like the fruit, therefore I heave at
the tree, or coveting to kiss the child, I therefore go about   20
to poison the teat.

Parmenio. Aye, but Clitus, I perceive you are born in the east,
and never laugh but at the sun rising, which argueth,
though a duty where you ought, yet no great devotion
where you might.   25

7-8 *son . . . Alexander is*] Philip of Macedon (382-336 BC), one of the most celebrated
military leaders of the Hellenic world, was succeeded by his son, Alexander (356-
323BC), who not only expanded his father's empire but also enriched the cultural
life of the lands he subdued.   13 *stain*] pun (diffuse tinted light on / reflect
adversely on)   13-15 *in the one . . . no comparison*] the tints of one (the turquoise)
may be compared, the transparency of the diamonds (being equal) cannot – hence
the equal excellence of Philip and Alexander.   18 *happily*] perhaps

Clitus. We will make no controversy of that which there
ought to be no question; only this shall be the opinion of
us both, that none was worthy to be the father of Alexander but Philip, nor any meet to be the son of Philip but
Alexander.   30
[*Enter*] TIMOCLEA, CAMPASPE [*and other captives, with spoils*].
Parmenio. Soft, Clitus, behold the spoils and prisoners, a
pleasant sight to us because profit is joined with honour,
not much painful to them because their captivity is eased
by mercy.
Timoclea. Fortune, thou didst never yet deceive virtue, 35
because virtue never yet did trust fortune. Sword and fire
will never get spoil where wisdom and fortitude bears
sway. O Thebes, thy walls were raised by the sweetness of
the harp, but razed by the shrillness of the trumpet.
Alexander had never come so near the walls had 40
Epaminondas walked about the walls, and yet might the
Thebans have been merry in their streets, if he had been to
watch their towers. But destiny is seldom foreseen, never
prevented. We are here now captives, whose necks are
yoked by force but whose hearts cannot yield by death. 45
Come, Campaspe and the rest, let us not be ashamed to
cast our eyes on him on whom we feared not to cast our
darts.
Parmenio. Madam, you need not doubt; it is Alexander that
is the conqueror.   50
Timoclea. Alexander hath overcome, not conquered.
Parmenio. To bring all under his subjection is to conquer.
Timoclea. He cannot subdue that which is divine.
Parmenio. Thebes was not.
Timoclea. Virtue is.   55
Clitus. Alexander, as he tendereth virtue, so he will you: he
drinketh not blood, but thirsteth after honour; he is greedy

38-9 *Thebes . . . harp*] Amphion, son of Zeus, fortified Thebes by playing on his
harp, causing the stones to raise themselves into walls. 41 *Epaminondas*] Theban
general and statesman distinguished for both his leadership and his integrity
(died 366 BC)

female: virginity/honor = fame

of victory, but never satisfied with mercy. In fight terrible,
as becometh a captain; in conquest mild, as beseemeth a
king. In all things, than which nothing can be greater, he is 60
Alexander.

Campaspe. Then, if it be such a thing to be Alexander, I hope
it shall be no miserable thing to be a virgin. For if he save
our honours, it is more than to restore our goods, and
rather do I wish he preserve our fame than our lives, 65
which if he do, we will confess there can be no greater
thing than to be Alexander.

       [*Enter*] ALEXANDER [*and*] HEPHESTION.

Alexander. Clitus, are these prisoners? Of whence these
spoils?

Clitus. Like your Majesty, they are prisoners, and of Thebes. 70

Alexander. Of what calling or reputation?

Clitus. I know not, but they seem to be ladies of honour.

Alexander. I will know. – Madam, of whence you are I know,
but who I cannot tell.

Timoclea. Alexander, I am the sister of Theagenes, who 75
fought a battle with thy father before the city of
Chaeronie; where he died – I say which none can gainsay
– valiantly.

Alexander. Lady, there seem in your words sparks of your
brother's deeds, but worser fortune in your life than his 80
death: but fear not, for you shall live without violence,
enemies, or necessity. But what are you, fair lady? Another
sister to Theagenes?

Campaspe. No sister to Theagenes, but an humble hand-
maid to Alexander, born of a mean parentage but to 85
extreme fortune.

Alexander. Well ladies, for so your virtues show you, whatsoever your births be, you shall be honourably entreated.
Athens shall be your Thebes, and you shall not be as
abjects of war but as subjects to Alexander. Parmenio, 90

58 *terrible*] inspiring terror 70 *Like your Majesty*] If it please your Majesty
75-7 *Theagenes . . . Chaeronie*] Theagenes, a leader of the Thebans resisting Philip
of Macedon, fell at Chaeronea in 338 BC. 85 *mean*] moderate 88 *entreated*]
treated 90 *abjects of*] those cast down by

conduct these honourable ladies into the city; charge the soldiers not so much as in words to offer them any offence, and let all wants be supplied so far forth as shall be necessary for such persons and my prisoners.

Exeunt PARMENIO *and captivi.*

Hephestion, it resteth now that we have as great care to govern in peace as conquer in war, that whilst arms cease, arts may flourish, and joining letters with lances we endeavour to be as good philosophers as soldiers, knowing it no less praise to be wise than commendable to be valiant.

Hephestion. Your Majesty therein showeth that you have as great desire to rule as to subdue, and needs must that commonwealth be fortunate whose captain is a philosopher, and whose philosopher is a captain.

Exeunt.

95

100

ACTUS PRIMUS SCAENA SECUNDA

[*Enter*] MANES, GRANICHUS, PSYLLUS.

Manes. I serve instead of a master, a mouse, whose house is a tub, whose dinner is a crust, and whose board is a bed.

Psyllus. Then art thou in a state of life which philosophers commend. A crumb for thy supper, an hand for thy cup, and thy clothes for thy sheets. For *Natura paucis contenta.*

Granichus. Manes, it is pity so proper a man should be cast away upon a philosopher; but that Diogenes, that dog, should have Manes, that dogbolt, it grieveth nature, and

5

---

2 *board*] table (in this case, the ground)   5 *Natura paucis contenta*] Nature is content with few things.   6 *proper*] handsome, well-proportioned   7 *Diogenes, that dog*] play on the meaning of Cynic (Greek, *kunikos*: 'dog-like'), the school of philosophy to which Diogenes belongs   8 *dogbolt*] contemptible wretch, dogsbody

spiteth art, the one having found thee so dissolute – absolute, I would say – in body, the other so single – singular – 10
in mind.

Manes. Are you merry? It is a sign by the trip of your tongue
and the toys of your head that you have done that today
which I have not done these three days.

Psyllus. What's that? 15

Manes. Dined.

Granichus. I think Diogenes keeps but cold cheer.

Manes. I would it were so, but he keepeth neither hot nor
cold.

Granichus. What then, lukewarm? That made Manes run 20
from his master last day.

Psyllus. Manes had reason, for his name foretold as much.

Manes. My name? How so, sir boy?

Psyllus. You know that it is called *Mons, a movendo*, because
it stands still? 25

Manes. Good.

Psyllus. And thou art named *Manes, a manendo*, because
thou runnest away.

Manes. Passing reasons! I did not run away, but retire.

Psyllus. To a prison, because thou wouldst have leisure to 30
contemplate.

Manes. I will prove that my body was immortal because it
was in prison.

Granichus. As how?

Manes. Did your masters never teach you that the soul is 35
immortal?

Granichus. Yes.

Manes. And the body is the prison of the soul?

Granichus. True.

Manes. Why then, thus: to make my body immortal I put 40
it to prison.

13 *toys*] idle fancies   21 *last day*] yesterday   24-8 *Mons . . . runnest away*] humor-
rous false etymology based on the principle of naming by opposition. Hence the
mountain is 'mons' from 'movendo' because it does not move, while Diogenes'
servant is 'Manes' from 'manendo' because he doesn't stay. (See Hunter (ed.),
Campaspe, I.ii. 24n and 27n, to which I am indebted.)   29 *passing*] excellent

Granichus. Oh, bad!

Psyllus. Excellent ill!

Manes. You may see how dull a fasting wit is. Therefore, Psyllus, let us go to supper with Granichus. Plato is the 45 best fellow of all philosophers. Give me him that reads in the morning in the school, and at noon in the kitchen.

Psyllus. And me.

Granichus. Ah sirs, my master is a king in his parlour for the body, and a god in his study for the soul. Among all 50 his men he commendeth one that is an excellent musician; then stand I by and clap another on the shoulder, and say, 'This is a passing good cook'.

Manes. It is well done, Granichus, for give me pleasure that goes in at the mouth, not the ear. I had rather fill my guts 55 than my brains.

Psyllus. I serve Apelles, who feedeth me as Diogenes doth Manes; for at dinner the one preacheth abstinence, the other commendeth counterfeiting. When I would eat meat, he paints a spit, and when I thirst, 'Oh', saith he, 'is 60 not this a fair pot?' and points to a table which contains the banquet of the gods, where are many dishes to feed the eye, but not to fill the gut.

Granichus. What dost thou then?

Psyllus. This doth he then: bring in many examples that 65 some have lived by savours, and proveth that much easier it is to fat by colours, and tells of birds that have been fat-ted by painted grapes in winter, and how many have so fed their eyes with their mistress' picture, that they never desired to take food, being glutted with the delight in their 70 favours. Then doth he show me counterfeits, such as have surfeited, with their filthy and loathsome vomits, and with the riotous bacchanals of the god Bacchus and his dis-orderly crew, which are painted all to the life in his shop.

59 *counterfeiting*] artistic representation, painting   61 *table*] pun (picture / dining board)   66 *by savours*] on smells   67 *fat*] grow fat   71-2 *Then doth he show . . . vomits*] cf. *Euphues*, p.7 above

77

To conclude, I fare hardly though I go richly, which 75
maketh me, when I should begin to shadow a lady's face,
to draw a lamb's head, and sometime to set to the body of
a maid a shoulder of mutton, for *semper animus meus est in
patinis.*

Manes.   Thou art a god to me, for could I see but a cook's 80
shop painted I would make mine eyes fat as butter. For I
have nought but sentences to fill my maw, as *plures occidit
crapula quam gladius, musa ieiunantibus amica*, 'repletion kil-
leth delicately', and (an old saw of abstinence) Socrates'
'The belly is the head's grave'. Thus with sayings, not with 85
meat, he maketh a gallimaufrey.

Granichus.   But how dost thou then live?

Manes.   With fine jests, sweet air, and the dog's alms.

Granichus.   Well, for this time I will staunch thy gut, and
among pots and platters thou shalt see what it is to serve 90
Plato.

Psyllus.   For joy of Granichus, let's sing.

Manes.   My voice is as clear in the evening as in the morning.

Granichus.   Another commodity of emptiness.

Song.

[*Granichus.   O for a bowl of fat canary,*   95
Rich Palermo, sparkling sherry!
Some nectar else from Juno's dairy,
O, these draughts would make us merry.

---

75 *fare hardly*] live barely (with a pun on fare: go / be fed   76 *shadow*] draw,
sketch   78-9 *semper . . . patinis*] my mind is always on the stew-pot.   80 *a god to
me*] a god in comparison with me   82 *sentences . . . maw*] maxims to satisfy my
stomach   82-3 *plures . . . amica*] more people are killed by surfeit than by the
sword, the Muse is friend to those who fast   86 *gallimaufrey*] hash (made of a
variety of meats)   88 *dog's alms*] scraps, with a pun on 'dog's' (Cynic's, i.e.
Diogenes')   94.1 *Song*] the song following the stage direction does not appear in
the Quarto. See Note on the Texts, p.xxiv above.   95 *canary*] a full-bodied wine
from the Canary Islands, popular in the sixteenth century   96 *Palermo*] a wine
from Sicily

Psyllus. O for a wench, I deal in faces,
   (And in other daintier things!)   100
   Tickled am I with her embraces,
   Fine dancing in such fairy rings.

Manes. O for a plump fat leg of mutton,
   Veal, lamb, capon, pig and coney!
   None is happy but a glutton,   105
   None an ass but who wants money.

Chorus. Wines, indeed, and girls are good,
   But brave victuals feast the blood.
   For wenches, wine and lusty cheer,
   Jove would leap down to surfeit here.]   110
                             [Exeunt].

ACTUS PRIMUS   SCAENA TERTIA

[Enter] MELIPPUS.

Melippus. I had never such ado to warn scholars to come
before a king. First I came to Chrysippus, a tall, lean, old,
mad man, willing him presently to appear before
Alexander. He stood staring on my face, neither moving
his eyes nor his body. I urging him to give some answer,   5
he took up a book, sat down, and said nothing. Melissa,
his maid, told me it was his manner, and that oftentimes
she was fain to thrust meat into his mouth, for that he
would rather starve than cease study. Well, thought I, seeing bookish men are so blockish, and so great clerks such 10
simple courtiers, I will neither be partaker of their commons nor their commendations. From thence I came

104 *coney*] rabbit
2 *Chrysippus*] Stoic philosopher (280-207 BC). His appearance in the play is
anachronistic. 10-11 *so great . . . courtiers*] such great scholars such unaccom-
plished courtiers 11-12 *commons*] provisions, rations

to Plato, and to Aristotle, and to divers other, none refus-
ing to come saving an old obscure fellow, who, sitting in a
tub turned towards the sun, read Greek to a young 15
boy. Him when I willed to appear before Alexander, he
answered, 'If Alexander would fain see me, let him come
to me; if learn of me, let him come to me; whatsoever it be,
let him come to me.' 'Why,' said I, 'he is a king.' He
answered, 'Why, I am a philosopher.' 'Why, but he is 20
Alexander.' 'Aye, but I am Diogenes.' I was half angry to
see one so crooked in his shape to be so crabbed in his sayings, so, going my way, I said, 'Thou shalt repent it if thou
comest not to Alexander.' 'Nay,' smiling answered he,
'Alexander may repent it if he come not to Diogenes. 25
Virtue must be sought, not offered.' And so, turning himself
to his cell, he grunted I know not what, like a pig under a
tub. But I must be gone; the philosophers are coming.

Exit.

[*Enter*] PLATO, ARISTOTLE, CHRYSIPPUS, CRATES, CLEANTHES,
ANAXARCHUS.

Plato. It is a difficult controversy, Aristotle, and rather to
be wondered at than believed, how natural causes should 30
work supernal effects.
Aristotle. I do not so much stand upon the apparition is seen
in the moon, neither the *demonium* of Socrates, as that I
cannot by natural reason give any reason of the ebbing

13 *Plato*] pupil of Socrates and originator of the doctrine of *ideas*. Since he died in
347 BC his appearance here is anachronistic. 13 *Aristotle*] See above, p.4n. 14-
16 *old obscure . . . boy*] Diogenes, identifiable for the audience through the reference to the tub in which he traditionally resided. 28.2-3 *Crates, Cleanthes,
Anaxarchus*] Greek philosophers. Crates of Athens held the chair of the Academy
c.270 BC. Cleanthes, his pupil, died c.220 BC from voluntary starvation.
Anaxarchus became a favourite of Alexander and followed him into Asia. 32-3 *I
do not . . . moon*] I do not rest my case principally on the face visible in the
moon. 33 *demonium of Socrates*] a divine voice which restrained the philosopher
(406-399 BC) and of which he was accustomed to speak in familiar terms.

and flowing of the sea, which makes me in the depth of 35
my studies to cry out, '*O ens entium miserere mei!*'

Plato. Cleanthes and you attribute so much to nature, by
searching for things which are not to be found, that, whilst
you study a cause of your own, you omit the occasion
itself. There is no man so savage in whom resteth not this 40
divine particle, that there is an omnipotent, eternal and
divine mover, which may be called God.

Cleanthes. I am of this mind, that that first mover, which
you term God, is the instrument of all the movings which
we attribute to nature. The earth, which is mass, swim- 45
meth on the sea; seasons divided in themselves, fruits
growing in themselves, the majesty of the sky, the whole
firmament of the world, and whatsoever else appeareth
miraculous, what man almost of mean capacity but can
prove it natural? 50

Anaxarchus. These causes shall be debated at our philosophers' feast, in which controversy I will take part with
Aristotle that there is *natura naturans*, and yet not God.

Crates. And I with Plato, that there is *Deus optimus maximus,*
and not nature. 55

Aristotle. Here cometh Alexander.

[*Enter*] ALEXANDER, HEPHESTION, PARMENIO, CLITUS.

Alexander. I see, Hephestion, that these philosophers are
here attending for us.

Hephestion. They were not philosophers if they knew not
their duties. 60

Alexander. But I much marvel Diogenes should be so
dogged.

Hephestion. I do not think but his excuse will be better than
Melippus' message.

---

36 *O ens entium miserere mei*] O thing of things have mercy on me.   40-1 *resteth
not . . . particle*] there does not reside some small element of this proposition concerning the divine.   49-50 *what man . . . natural*] is there any man, even of moderate intellect, who cannot show it to be natural?   53 *natura naturans*] a natural
force from which everything in nature springs   54 *Deus optimus maximus*] God,
the greatest and highest   63 *I do not think but*] I imagine that

Alexander. I will go see him, Hephestion, because I long to 65
see him that would command Alexander to come, to
whom all the world is like to come. – Aristotle and the rest,
sithence my coming from Thebes to Athens, from a place
of conquest to a palace of quiet, I have resolved with
myself in my court to have as many philosophers as I had 70
in my camp soldiers. My court shall be a school, wherein
I will have used as great doctrine in peace as I did in war
discipline.

Aristotle. We are all here ready to be commanded, and glad
we are that we are commanded, for that nothing better 75
becometh kings than literature, which maketh them come
as near to the gods in wisdom as they do in dignity.

Alexander. It is so, Aristotle; but yet there is among you,
yea, and of your bringing up, that sought to destroy
Alexander – Callisthenes, Aristotle, whose treasons 80
against his prince shall not be borne out with the reasons
of his philosophy.

Aristotle. If ever mischief entered into the heart of Callisthenes, let Callisthenes suffer for it; but that Aristotle ever
imagined any such thing of Callisthenes, Aristotle doth 85
deny.

Alexander. Well, Aristotle, kindred may blind thee, and
affection me, but in king's causes I will not stand to
scholars' arguments. This meeting shall be for a commandment that you all frequent my court, instruct the 90
young with rules, confirm the old with reasons. Let your
lives be answerable to your learnings, lest my proceedings
be contrary to my promises.

Hephestion. You said you would ask every one of them a
question, which yesternight none of us could answer.   95

Alexander. I will. – Plato, of all beasts which is the subtlest?

Plato. That which man hitherto never knew.

Alexander. Aristotle, how should a man be thought a god?

---

72 *used*] practised   80 *Callisthenes*] pupil of Aristotle, initially favoured by
Alexander but so outspoken that he fell into disgrace   88 *stand to*] accede to,
yield to   92 *answerable to*] in accordance with

Aristotle. In doing a thing unpossible for a man.

Alexander. Chrysippus, which was first, the day or the 100
night?

Chrysippus. The day, by a day.

Alexander. Indeed, strange questions must have strange
answers. Cleanthes, what say you, is life or death the
stronger? 105

Cleanthes. Life, that suffereth so many troubles.

Alexander. Crates, how long should a man live?

Crates. Till he think it better to die than live.

Alexander. Anaxarchus, whether doth the sea or the earth
bring forth most creatures? 110

Anaxarchus. The earth, for the sea is but a part of the earth.

Alexander. Hephestion, methinks they have answered all
well, and in such questions I mean often to try them.

Hephestion. It is better to have in your court a wise man
than in your ground a golden mine. Therefore would I 115
leave war to study wisdom, were I Alexander.

Alexander. So would I, were I Hephestion. But come, let us
go and give release, as I promised, to our Theban thralls.

     Exeunt [ALEXANDER, HEPHESTION, CLITUS, PARMENIO].

Plato. Thou art fortunate, Aristotle, that Alexander is thy
scholar. 120

Aristotle. And all you happy that he is your sovereign.

Chrysippus. I could like the man well, if he could be contented to be but a man.

Aristotle. He seeketh to draw near to the gods in knowledge, not to be a god. 125

     [DIOGENES *is discovered at his tub.*]

Plato. Let us question a little with Diogenes, why he went
not with us to Alexander. – Diogenes, thou didst forget thy
duty that thou went'st not with us to the king.

Diogenes. And you your profession, that you went to the
king. 130

Plato. Thou takest as great pride to be peevish as others do
glory to be virtuous.

131 *peevish*] perverse

Diogenes. And thou as great honour, being a philosopher, to be thought court-like as others shame, that be courtiers, to be accounted philosophers.   135

Aristotle. These austere manners set aside, it is well known that thou didst counterfeit money.

Diogenes. And thou thy manners, in that thou didst not counterfeit money.

Aristotle. Thou hast reason to contemn the court, being both 140 in body and mind too crooked for a courtier.

Diogenes. As good be crooked and endeavour to make myself straight from the court, as to be straight and learn to be crooked at the court.

Crates. Thou thinkest it a grace to be opposite against 145 Alexander.

Diogenes. And thou to be jump with Alexander.

Anaxarchus. Let us go; for in contemning him we shall better please him than in wondering at him.

[*They move away.*]

Aristotle. Plato, what dost thou think of Diogenes?   150

Plato. To be Socrates furious. Let us go.

Exeunt philosophi.

138-9 *And thou . . . money*] And you your morality in that you did not forge [anything as trivial as] money (i.e. they compromised their virtue more profoundly by their demeanour towards Alexander). 140 *contemn*] scorn 147 *jump with*] in agreement with 151 *furious*] mad

Actus Secundus

DIOGENES [*rediscovered at his tub, with a lantern*].
[*Enter*] PSYLLUS, MANES, GRANICHUS.

Psyllus.   Behold, Manes, where thy master is, seeking either
  for bones for his dinner or pins for his sleeves. I will go
  salute him.

Manes.   Do so. But, mum! – not a word that you saw Manes.

Granichus.   Then stay thou behind, and I will go with Psyllus.   5
  [PSYLLUS *and* GRANICHUS *approach* DIOGENES.]

Psyllus.   All hail, Diogenes, to your proper person.

Diogenes.   All hate to thy peevish conditions.

Granichus.   Oh, dog!

Psyllus.   What dost thou seek for here?

Diogenes.   For a man and a beast.   10

Granichus.   That is easy without thy light to be found. Be
  not all these men?

Diogenes.   Called men.

Granichus.   What beast is it thou lookest for?

Diogenes.   The beast my man, Manes.   15

Psyllus.   He is a beast indeed that will serve thee.

Diogenes.   So is he that begat thee.

Granichus.   What wouldst thou do if thou shouldst find
  Manes?

Diogenes.   Give him leave to do as he hath done before.   20

Granichus.   What's that?

Diogenes.   To run away.

Psyllus.   Why, hast thou no need of Manes?

Diogenes.   It were a shame for Diogenes to have need of
  Manes, and for Manes to have no need of Diogenes.   25

Granichus.   But put the case he were gone, wouldst thou
  entertain any of us two?

Diogenes.   Upon condition.

6 *proper person*] pun (you yourself / handsome form)   26 *put the case*] suppose
27 *entertain*] employ

Psyllus. What?

Diogenes. That you should tell me wherefore any of you 30
 both were good.

Granichus. Why, I am a scholar and well seen in philosphy.

Psyllus. And I a prentice and well seen in painting.

Diogenes. Well then, Granichus, be thou a painter to amend
 thine ill face, and thou, Psyllus, a philosopher to correct 35
 thine evil manners. – But who is that? Manes?

Manes. I care not who I were, so I were not Manes.

Granichus [to Manes]. You are taken tardy.

Psyllus [to Granichus]. Let us slip aside, Granichus, to see
 the salutation between Manes and his master. 40

Diogenes. Manes, thou knowest the last day I threw away
 my dish to drink in my hand, because it was superfluous.
 Now I am determined to put away my man and serve
 myself, *quia non egeo tui vel te.*

Manes. Master, you know a while ago I ran away; so do I 45
 mean to do again, *quia scio tibi non esse argentum.*

Diogenes. I know I have no money, neither will I have ever
 a man. For I was resolved long sithence to put away both
 my slaves – money and Manes.

Manes. So was I determined to shake off both my dogs – 50
 hunger and Diogenes.

Psyllus [to Granichus]. O sweet consent between a crowd
 and a jew's harp.

Granichus [to Psyllus]. Come, let us reconcile them.

Psyllus [to Granichus]. It shall not need, for this is their use. 55
 Now do they dine one upon another.

                    Exit DIOG[ENES].

---

33 *seen in*] informed about, grounded in   38 *taken tardy*] caught unawares (cf.
caught napping)   44 *quia non egeo tui vel te*] because I do not need you   46 *quia
scio tibi non esse argentum*] because I know you have no money   47-8 *neither . . .
man*] and I will not have a servant either   52 *consent*] musical agreement   52-3
crowd / jew's harp] fiddle / small musical instrument held in the mouth and
played with one finger (i.e. two instruments with nothing in common)   55 *use*]
customary behaviour

86

Granichus. How now, Manes, art thou gone from thy master?

Manes. No, I did but now bind myself to him.

Psyllus. Why, you were at mortal jars.

Manes. In faith, no; we brake a bitter jest one upon another. 60

Granichus. Why, thou art as dogged as he.

Psyllus. My father knew them both little whelps.

Manes. Well, I will hie me after my master.

Granichus. Why, is it supper time with Diogenes?

Manes. Aye, with him at all times when he hath meat. 65

Psyllus. Why then, every man to his home, and let us steal
out again anon.

Granichus. Where shall we meet?

Psyllus. Why, at *alae vendibili suspensa haedera non est opus.*

Manes. Oh, Psyllus, *habeo te loco parentis.* Thou blessest me! 70

Exeunt.

ACTUS SECUNDAS   SCAENA SECUNDA

[*Enter*] ALEXANDER, HEPHESTION, PAGE.

Alexander. Stand aside, sir boy, till you be called. – Hephestion, how do ye like the sweet face of Campaspe?

Hephestion. I cannot but commend the stout courage of
Timoclea.

Alexander. Without doubt Campaspe had some great man 5
to her father.

Hephestion. You know Timoclea had Theagenes to her
brother.

Alexander. Timoclea still in thy mouth! Art thou not in love?

Hephestion. Not I. 10

---

59 *at . . . jars*] in deadly conflict   69 *alae . . . opus*] an ale house. The Latin tag is
a variation on the proverb 'a good wine needs no bush' (i.e. a tavern selling good
wine needs no advertisement) with 'ale' replacing 'wine'.   70 *habeo . . . parentis*] I
have you in place of a parent.

Alexander. Not with Timoclea, you mean, wherein you
resemble the lapwing, who crieth most where her nest is
not. And so you lead me from espying your love with
Campaspe: you cry 'Timoclea'.

Hephestion. Could I as well subdue kingdoms as I can my 15
thoughts, or were I as far from ambition as I am from love,
all the world would account me as valiant in arms as I
know myself moderate in affection.

Alexander. Is love a vice?

Hephestion. It is no virtue. 20

Alexander. Well, now shalt thou see what small difference
I make between Alexander and Hephestion. And sith thou
hast been always partaker of my triumphs, thou shalt be
partaker of my torments. I love, Hephestion, I love! I love
Campaspe, a thing far unfit for a Macedonian, for a king, 25
for Alexander. Why hangest thou down thy head,
Hephestion, blushing to hear that which I am not
ashamed to tell?

Hephestion. Might my words crave pardon and my counsel
credit, I would both discharge the duty of a subject, for so 30
I am, and the office of a friend, for so I will.

Alexander. Speak Hephestion, for whatsoever is spoken,
Hephestion speaketh to Alexander.

Hephestion. I cannot tell, Alexander, whether the report be
more shameful to be heard or the cause sorrowful to be 35
believed. What, is the son of Philip, King of Macedon,
become the subject of Campaspe, the captive of Thebes? Is
that mind, whose greatness the world could not contain,
drawn within the compass of an idle, alluring eye? Will
you handle the spindle with Hercules, when you 40
should shake the spear with Achilles? Is the warlike sound
of drum and trump turned to the soft noise of lyre and

12-13 *lapwing . . . not*] a reference to the lapwing's strategy for drawing predators
from its nest by calling and running in another direction. 25 *Macedonian*] traditionally a war-like people 40 *spindle with Hercules*] a common comparison
denoting the degenerative nature of love. Hercules, having fallen in love with
Omphale, dressed as a woman to please her and worked at a spinning wheel.

lute, the neighing of barbed steeds, whose loudness filled
the air with terror, and whose breaths dimmed the sun
with smoke, converted to delicate tunes and 45
amorous glances? Oh, Alexander! That soft and yielding
mind should not be in him whose hard and unconquered
heart hath made so many yield. But you love! Ah, grief!
But whom? Campaspe! Ah, shame! A maid forsooth,
unknown, unnoble, and who can tell whether immodest, 50
whose eyes are framed by art to enamour and whose heart
was made by nature to enchant. Aye, but she is beautiful!
Yea, but not therefore chaste. Aye, but she is comely in all
parts of the body! Yea, but she may be crooked in some
part of the mind. Aye, but she is wise. Yea, but she is a 55
woman! Beauty is like the blackberry, which seemeth red
when it is not ripe, resembling precious stones that are
polished with honey, which, the smoother they look, the
sooner they break. It is thought wonderful among the sea-
men that mugil, of all fishes the swiftest, is found in the 60
belly of the bret, of all the slowest, and shall it not seem
monstrous to wise men that the heart of the greatest conqueror of the world should be found in the hands of the
weakest creature of nature – of a woman, of a captive?
Ermines have fair skins but foul livers, sepulchres fresh 65
colours but rotten bones, women fair faces but false hearts.
Remember, Alexander, thou hast a camp to govern, not a
chamber; fall not from the armour of Mars to the arms of
Venus, from the fiery assaults of war to the maidenly skirmishes of love, from displaying the eagle in thine ensign 70
to set down the sparrow. I sigh, Alexander, that where fortune could not conquer, folly should overcome. But
behold all the perfection that may be in Campaspe – a hair
curling by nature not art, sweet alluring eyes, a fair face
made in despite of Venus and a stately port in disdain of 75
Juno, a wit apt to conceive and quick to answer, a skin as

43 *barbed*] caparisoned for battle   60-1 *mugil / bret*] mullet / turbot   68-9 *Mars /
Venus*] god of war / goddess of love   70-1 *eagle / sparrow*] emblems of war /
lechery   75 *in despite of Venus*] in defiance of Venus' jealous disapproval   75-
6 *in disdain of Juno*] to disparage that of the Queen of the gods

89

soft as silk and as smooth as jet, a long white hand, a fine little foot, to conclude, all parts answerable to the best part – what of this? Though she have heavenly gifts, virtue and beauty, is she not of earthly metal, flesh and blood? You, 80 Alexander, that would be a god, show yourself in this worse than a man, so soon to be both overseen and overtaken in a woman, whose false tears know their true times, whose smooth words wound deeper than sharp swords. There is no surfeit so dangerous as that of honey, nor any 85 poison so deadly as that of love; in the one physic cannot prevail, nor in the other counsel.

Alexander. My case were light, Hephestion, and not worthy to be called love, if reason were a remedy or sentences could salve that sense cannot conceive. Little do you 90 know, and therefore slightly do you regard, the dead embers in a private person or live coals in a great prince, whose passions and thoughts do as far exceed others in extremity as their callings do in majesty. An eclipse in the sun is more than the falling of a star; none can conceive the 95 torments of a king unless he be a king, whose desires are not inferior to their dignities. And then judge, Hephestion, if the agonies of love be dangerous in a subject, whether they be not more than deadly unto Alexander, whose deep and not-to-be-conceived sighs cleave the heart in 100 shivers, whose wounded thoughts can neither be expressed nor endured. Cease then, Hephestion, with arguments to seek to refel that which with their deity the gods cannot resist, and let this suffice to answer thee, that it is a king that loveth, and Alexander, whose affections 105 are not to be measured by reason, being immortal, nor (I fear me) to be borne, being intolerable.

Hephestion. I must needs yield, when neither reason nor counsel can be heard.

82-3 *overseen and overtaken in*] deceived and captivated by   88 *my case were light*] my situation would not be grave   89 *sentences*] proverbial wisdom   90 *salve*] soothe   103 *refel*] counter, repel

90

Alexander. Yield, Hephestion, for Alexander doth love and 110
therefore must obtain.

Hephestion. Supppose she loves not you. Affection cometh
not by appointment or birth, and then as good hated as
enforced.

Alexander. I am a king and will command. 115

Hephestion. You may, to yield to lust by force; but to consent
to love by fear, you cannot.

Alexander. Why, what is that which Alexander may not
conquer as he list?

Hephestion. Why, that which you say the gods cannot resist. 120
Love.

Alexander. I am a conqueror, she a captive; I as fortunate as
she fair. My greatness may answer her wants, and the
gifts of my mind the modesty of hers. Is it not likely, then,
that she should love? Is it not reasonable? 125

Hephestion. You say that in love there is no reason, and
therefore there can be no likelihood.

Alexander. No more, Hephestion. In this case I will use
mine own counsel, and in all other thine advice. Thou
mayest be a good soldier, but never good lover. Call my 130
page.

[PAGE *approaches.*]

Sirrah, go presently to Apelles, and will him to come to
me without either delay or excuse.

Page. I go.

[*Exit* PAGE.]

Alexander. In the mean season, to recreate my spirits, being 135
so near, we will go see Diogenes. [Diogenes' *tub is discov-
ered.*] And see where his tub is. – Diogenes!

Diogenes. Who calleth?

Alexander. Alexander.

DIOGENES [*emerges.*]

How happened it that you would not come out of your 140
tub to my palace?

Diogenes. Because it was as far from my tub to your palace
as from your palace to my tub.

Alexander. Why then, dost thou owe no reverence to kings?

Diogenes.   No.   145
Alexander.   Why so?
Diogenes.   Because they be no gods.
Alexander.   They be gods of the earth.
Diogenes.   Yea, gods of earth.
Alexander.   Plato is not of thy mind.   150
Diogenes.   I am glad of it.
Alexander.   Why?
Diogenes.   Because I would have none of Diogenes' mind
but Diogenes.
Alexander.   If Alexander have anything that may pleasure 155
Diogenes, let me know, and take it.
Diogenes.   Then take not from me that you cannot give me,
the light of the world.
Alexander.   What dost thou want?
Diogenes.   Nothing that you have.   160
Alexander.   I have the world at command.
Diogenes.   And I in contempt.
Alexander.   Thou shalt live no longer than I will.
Diogenes.   But I shall die whether you will or no.
Alexander.   How should one learn to be content?   165
Diogenes.   Unlearn to covet.
Alexander.   Hephestion, were I not Alexander, I would wish
to be Diogenes.
Hephestion.   He is dogged, but discrete. I cannot tell how –
sharp, with a kind of sweetness; full of wit, yet too, too 170
wayward.
Alexander.   Diogenes, when I come this way again I will
both see thee and confer with thee.
Diogenes.   Do.   [*Withdraws into his tub.*]
                    [*Enter*] APELLES.
Alexander.   But here cometh Apelles. How now, Apelles, is 175
Venus' face yet finished?

157-8 *Then take . . . world*] i.e. Alexander is obscuring the light in standing before
Diogenes   163 *Thou shalt . . . will*] ambiguous. 'Your life will be no longer than
mine / I can end your life when I wish.' Diogenes plays on the latter meaning.   169 *dogged, but discrete*] currish / typical of a Cynic, but judicious

Apelles. Not yet. Beauty is not so soon shadowed, whose
perfection cometh not within the compass either of cunning or of colour.
Alexander. Well, let it rest unperfect; and come you with 180
me, where I will show you that finished by nature that you
have been trifling about by art.

[*Exeunt*]

Actus Tertius

SCAENA PRIMA

[*Enter*] APELLES, CAMPASPE [*with* PSYLLUS].

Apelles. Lady, I doubt whether there be any colour so fresh
that may shadow a countenance so fair.
Campaspe. Sir, I had thought you had been commanded to
paint with your hand, not to gloze with your tongue; but,
as I have heard, it is the hardest thing in painting to set 5
down a hard favour, which maketh you to despair of my
face, and then shall you have as great thanks to spare your
labour as to discredit your art.
Apelles. Mistress, you neither differ from yourself nor your
sex; for, knowing your own perfection, you seem to dis- 10
praise that which men most commend, drawing them by
that mean into an admiration, where, feeding themselves,
they fall into an ecstasy, your modesty being the cause of
the one, and of the other, your affections.

178-9 *cunning*] skill
6 *hard favour*] unlovely countenance   14 *affections*] disposition

93

Campaspe. I am too young to understand your speech, 15
   though old enough to withstand your device. You have
   been so long used to colours, you can do nothing but
   colour.
Apelles. Indeed, the colours I see, I fear, will alter the colour
   I have. But come, madam, will you draw near? For 20
   Alexander will be here anon. – Psyllus, stay you here at
   the window. If any enquire for me, answer *'Non lubet esse*
   domi.'

   Exeunt [APELLES *and* CAMPASPE *into Apelles' shop*].

ACTUS TERTIUS   SCAENA SECUNDA

PSYLLUS [*remains behind*].

Psyllus. It is always my master's fashion, when any fair
   gentlewoman is to be drawn within, to make me to stay
   without. But if he should paint Jupiter like a bull, like a
   swan, like an eagle, then must Psyllus with one hand
   grind colours, and with the other hold the candle. But let 5
   him alone; the better he shadows her face, the more will he
   burn his own heart. And now if a man could meet with
   Manes, who, I dare say, looks as lean as if Diogenes
   dropped out of his nose.

   [*Enter*] MANES.

Manes. And here comes Manes, who hath as much meat in 10
   his maw as thou hast honesty in thy head.
Psyllus. Then I hope thou art very hungry.
Manes. They that know thee, know that.

---

18 *colour*] pun (paint / embellish the truth)   19-20 *colours I see . . . colour I have*]
the complexion I look at will, I fear, bring the colour to (or drain it from) my own
face.   22 *window*] i.e. of the workshop   22-3 *Non lubet esse domi*] It does not
please him to be at home.
9 *dropped out of his nose*] proverbial expression for hunger

94

Psyllus. But dost thou not remember that we have certain
    liquor to confer withal?   15
Manes. Aye, but I have business. I must go cry a thing.
Psyllus. Why, what hast thou lost?
Manes. That which I never had, my dinner.
Psyllus. Foul lubber, wilt thou cry for thy dinner?
Manes. I mean, I must cry – not as one would say 'cry', but 20
    'cry', that is, make a noise.
Psyllus. Why, fool, that is all one; for if thou cry thou must
    needs make a noise.
Manes. Boy, thou art deceived. 'Cry' hath divers significa-
    tions, and may be alluded to many things; 'knave' but 25
    one, and can be applied but to thee.
Psyllus. Profound Manes!
Manes. We Cynics are mad fellows. Didst thou not find I
    did quip thee?
Psyllus. No, verily. Why, what's a quip?   30
Manes. We great girders call it a short saying of a sharp wit,
    with a bitter sense in a sweet word.
Psyllus. How canst thou thus divine, divide, define, dispute,
    and all on the sudden?
Manes. Wit will have his swing; I am bewitched, inspired, 35
    inflamed, infected.
Psyllus. Well, then will not I tempt thy jibing spirit.
Manes. Do not, Psyllus, for thy dull head will be but a
    grindstone for my quick wit, which, if thou whet with
    overthwarts, *periisti, actum est de te*. I have drawn blood 40
    at one's brains with a bitter bob.
Psyllus. Let me cross myself; for I die if I cross thee.
Manes. Let me do my business. I myself am afraid lest my
    wit should wax warm, and then must it needs consume
    some hard head with fine and pretty jests. I am sometimes 45

16 *cry a thing*] make a proclamation about something 20-1 *cry, but cry*] weep,
but shout 31 *girders*] scoffers, cavillers 31 *wit*] intelligence 40 *overthwarts*]
contradictions 40 *periisti, actum est de te*] you have perished, you have had
it 41 *one's*] someone's 41 *bitter bob*] sharp taunt 42 *cross myself / cross
thee*] make the sign of the cross (i.e. bless myself) / oppose you

the god who binds the winds in the hollows of the earth that he caused the seas to break their bounds, sith men 30 had broke their vows, and to swell as far above their reach as men had swerved beyond their reason. Then might you see ships sail where sheep fed, anchors cast where ploughs go, fishermen throw their nets where husbandmen sow their corn, and fishes throw their scales where 35 fowls do breed their quills. Then might you gather froth where now is dew, rotten weeds for sweet roses, and take view of monstrous mermaids instead of passing fair maids.

Gallathea. To hear these sweet marvels, I would mine eyes 40 were turned also into ears.

Tyterus. But at the last, our countrymen repenting, and not too late because at last, Neptune, either weary of his wrath, or wary to do them wrong, upon condition consented to ease their miseries. 45

Gallathea. What condition will not miserable men accept?

Tyterus. The condition was this, that at every five years' day the fairest and chastest virgin in all the country should be brought unto this tree, and here being bound, whom neither parentage shall excuse for honour nor 50 virtue for integrity, is left for a peace offering unto Neptune.

Gallathea. Dear is the peace that is bought with guiltless ✗ blood.

Tyterus. I am not able to say that; but he sendeth a monster 55 called the *Agar*, against whose coming the waters roar, the fowls fly away, and the cattle in the field for terror shun the banks.

Gallathea. And she bound to endure that horror?

Tyterus. And she bound to endure that horror. 60

---

30 *sith*] since   36 *quills*] feathers   38 *mermaids*] Modern spelling (for Quarto 'maremaids') obscures the rhyme with 'fair maids' (lines 38-9).   38-9 *passing fair maids*] pun. Both 'maidens who pass by' and 'young women of surpassing beauty'. 56 *Agar*] personification of the 'eagre', the tidal bore on the Humber estuary   57 *fowls*] birds   59-60 *bound / bound*] pun (obliged / tied up)

135

Gallathea. Doth this monster devour her?

Tyterus. Whether she be devoured of him, or conveyed to
Neptune, or drowned between both, it is not permitted to
know, and incurreth danger to conjecture. Now, Gallathea,
here endeth my tale, and beginneth thy tragedy.   65

Gallathea. Alas, father, and why so?

Tyterus. I would thou hadst been less fair or more fortunate,
then shouldst thou not repine that I have disguised thee in
this attire; for thy beauty will make thee to be thought worthy of this god. To avoid, therefore, destiny (for wisdom   70
ruleth the stars), I think it better to use an unlawful means,
your honour preserved, than intolerable grief, both life
and honour hazarded, and to prevent, if it be possible, thy
constellation by my craft. Now hast thou heard the custom
of this country, the cause why this tree was dedicated unto   75
Neptune, and the vexing care of thy fearful father.

Gallathea. Father, I have been attentive to hear and, by your
patience, am ready to answer. Destiny may be deferred,
not prevented, and therefore it were better to offer myself
in triumph than to be drawn to it with dishonour. Hath   80
Nature, as you say, made me so fair above all, and shall
not virtue make me as famous as others? Do you not
know, or doth over-carefulness make you forget, that an
honourable death is to be preferred before an infamous
life? I am but a child, and have not lived long, and yet not 85
so childish as I desire to live ever. Virtues I mean to carry
to my grave, not grey hairs. I would I were as sure that
destiny would light on me as I am resolved it could not
fear me. Nature hath given me beauty; virtue, courage:
Nature must yield me death; virtue, honour. Suffer me,   90
therefore, to die, for which I was born; or let me curse that
I was born, sith I may not die for it.

Tyterus. Alas, Gallathea, to consider the causes of change

---

74 *constellation . . . craft*] forestall, if possible, through my cunning, the destiny
ordained by the disposition of the stars at the time of your
birth 76 *fearful*] apprehensive 89 *fear me*] make me afraid 90 *Suffer
me*] permit me

136

thou art too young, and that I should find them out for (?)
thee, too, too fortunate.   95
Gallathea.   The destiny to me cannot be so hard as the dis-
guising hateful.
Tyterus.   To gain love the gods have taken shapes of beasts,
and to save life art thou coy to take the attire of men?
Gallathea.   They were beastly gods, that lust could make 100
them seem as beasts.
Tyterus.   In health it is easy to counsel the sick, but it's hard
for the sick to follow wholesome counsel. Well, let us
depart; the day is far spent.

Exeunt.

(handwritten: a serious enditement of classical "godly" behavior.)

(handwritten: is G. "sick" with her desire to be virtuous?)

ACTUS PRIMUS   SCAENA SECUNDA

[*Enter*] CUPID, NYMPH *of Diana.*
Cupid.   Fair nymph, are you strayed from your company by
chance, or love you to wander solitarily on purpose?
Nymph.   Fair boy, or god, or whatever you be, I would you
knew these woods are to me so well known that I cannot
stray though I would, and my mind so free that to be   5
melancholy I have no cause. There is none of Diana's train
that any can train, either out of their way or out of their
wits.
Cupid.   What is that Diana, a goddess? What her nymphs,
virgins? What her pastimes, hunting?   10
Nymph.   A goddess? Who knows it not? Virgins? Who
thinks it not? Hunting? Who loves it not?

98 *gods . . . beasts*] A number of classical deities assumed the form of animals in
order to pursue mortal women (cf. Jupiter's rape of Leda in the form of a swan).
99 *coy*] diffident, too scrupulous
6-7 *train / train*] followers / lure

137

Cupid. I pray thee, sweet wench, amongst all your sweet troop is there not one that followeth the sweetest thing, sweet love? 15

Nymph. Love, good sir? What mean you by it? Or what do you call it?

Cupid. A heat full of coldness, a sweet full of bitterness, a pain full of pleasantness, which maketh thoughts have eyes, and hearts ears. Bred by desire, nursed by delight, 20 weaned by jealousy, killed by dissembling, buried by ingratitude. And this is love. Fair lady, will you any?

Nymph. If it be nothing else, it is but a foolish thing.

Cupid. Try, and you shall find it a pretty thing.

Nymph. I have neither will nor leisure, but I will follow 25 Diana in the chase, whose virgins are all chaste, delighting in the bow that wounds the swift hart in the forest, not fearing the bow that strikes the soft heart in the chamber. This difference is between my mistress, Diana, and your mother (as I guess), Venus, that all her nymphs are ami- 30 able and wise in their kind, the other amorous and too kind for their sex. And so farewell, little god. *Exit.*

Cupid. Diana, and thou, and all thine, shall know that Cupid is a great god. I will practise awhile in these woods, and play such pranks with these nymphs that while they 35 aim to hit others with their arrows they shall be wounded themselves with their own eyes.

Exit.

31-2 *kind / kind*] by nature / liberal in affection   34 *awhile*] pun on 'a wile' (i.e. a trick) and 'awhile' (i.e. for a time)

[*Enter*] MELEBEUS, PHILLIDA.

Melebeus. Come, Phillida, fair Phillida, and (I fear me) too
fair, being my Phillida. Thou knowest the custom of this
country, and I the greatness of thy beauty; we both the
fierceness of the monster, *Agar*. Everyone thinketh his own
child fair, but I know that which I most desire and   5
would least have, that thou art fairest. Thou shalt therefore disguise thyself in attire, lest I should disguise myself
in affection, in suffering thee to perish by a fond desire,
whom I may preserve by a sure deceit.

Phillida. Dear father, Nature could not make me so fair as   10
she hath made you kind, nor you more kind than me duti-
ful. Whatsoever you command I will not refuse, because
you command nothing but my safety and your happiness.
But how shall I be disguised?

Melebeus. In man's apparel.   15

Phillida. It will neither become my body nor my mind.

Melebeus. Why, Phillida?

Phillida. For then I must keep company with boys, and
commit follies unseemly for my sex, or keep company
with girls, and be thought more wanton than becometh   20
me. Besides, I shall be ashamed of my long hose and short
coat, and so unwarily blab out something by blushing at
everything.

Melebeus. Fear not, Phillida. Use will make it easy; fear
must make it necessary.   25

Phillida. I agree, since my father will have it so, and fortune
must.

Melebeus. Come, let us in, and when thou art disguised
roam about these woods till the time be past and Neptune
pleased.   30

Exeunt.

8 *fond*] foolish

[*Enter*] Mariner, Rafe, Robin, *and* Dick.

Robin. Now, Mariner, what callest thou this sport on the
  sea?

Mariner. It is called a wrack.

Rafe. I take no pleasure in it. Of all deaths, I would not be
  drowned; one's clothes will be so wet when he is taken up. 5

Dick. What call'st thou the thing we were bound to?

Mariner. A rafter.

Rafe. I will rather hang myself on a rafter in the house than
  be so haled in the sea; there one may have a leap for his
  life. But I marvel how our master speeds.   10

Dick. I'll warrant by this time he is wet-shod. Did you ever
  see water bubble as the sea did? But what shall we do?

Mariner. You are now in Lincolnshire, where you can want
  no fowl, if you can devise means to catch them. There be
  woods hard by, and at every mile's end houses: so that if 15
  you seek on the land, you shall speed better than on the
  sea.

Robin. Sea? Nay, I will never sail more. I brook not their
  diet. Their bread is so hard that one must carry a whetstone in his mouth to grind his teeth, the meat so salt that 20
  one would think after dinner his tongue had been pow-
  dered ten days.

Rafe. Oh, thou hast a sweet life, Mariner, to be pinned in a
  few boards, and to be within an inch of a thing bottom-
  less. I pray thee, how often hast thou been drowned?   25

Mariner. Fool, thou seest I am yet alive.

Robin. Why, be they dead that be drowned? I had thought
  they had been with the fish, and so by chance been caught
  up with them in a net again. It were a shame a little cold
  water should kill a man of reason, when you shall see a   30
  poor minnow lie in it that hath no understanding.

6 *bound to*] echo of I.i.59-60 10 *marvel*] wonder 10 *speeds*] fares 13 *want*]
lack 18 *brook not*] cannot endure 19-20 *whetstone*] shaped stone used for
sharpening tools

Mariner. Thou art wise from the crown of thy head upwards `.`
Seek you new fortunes now: I will follow mine old. I can
shift the moon and the sun, and know by one card what
all you cannot do by a whole pair. The loadstone that 35
always holdeth his nose to the north, the two and thirty
points for the wind: the wonders I see would make all you
blind. You be but boys. I fear the sea no more than a dish
of water. Why, fools, it is but a liquid element. Farewell.
> *[Moves away.]*
Robin. It were good we learned his cunning at the cards, for 40
we must live by cozenage. We have neither lands, nor wit,
nor masters, nor honesty.
Rafe. Nay, I would fain have his thirty-two – that is his
three dozen lacking four – points, for you see betwixt us
three there is not two good points. 45
Dick. Let us call him a little back, that we may learn those
points. *[To the Mariner.]* Sirrah, a word. I pray thee, show
us thy points.
Mariner [returning]. Will you learn?
Dick. Aye. 50
Mariner. Then, as you like this, I will instruct you in all our
secrets, for there is not a clout, nor card, nor board, nor
post that hath not a special name or singular nature.
Dick. Well, begin with your points, for I lack only points in
this world. 55
Mariner. North. North and by east. North-north-east.
North-east and by north. North-east. North-east and by
east. East-north-east. East and by north. East.

---

34 *shift*] record the variations in the position of   34 *card*] shipman's card, a cir-
cular piece of stiff paper marking the thirty-two points of the compass   35 *pair*]
pack (with a pun on 'card', i.e. shipman's card / playing card)   35-6 *loadstone . . .
north*] magnet which always points to the north   36-7 *two and thirty . . . wind*] the
compass points by which to determine the direction of the wind. The term 'point'
also signifies the tagged lace used for fastening hose, hence Rafe's confusion at
line 44ff.   40 *cards*] Misunderstanding by Robin of the term 'card', which he
takes as 'playing card'.   41 *cozenage*] cheating, trickery   52 *clout*] sail   53 *singular*] particular

Dick. I'll say it. North. North-east. North-east. Nore-nore
and by nore-east. I shall never do it!   60
Mariner. This is but one quarter.
Robin. I shall never learn a quarter of it. I will try. North.
North-east is by the west side. North and by north.
Dick. Passing ill.
Mariner. Hast thou no memory? Try thou.   65
Rafe. North-north and by north. I can go no further.
Mariner. Oh dullard! Is thy head lighter than the wind and
thy tongue so heavy it will not wag? I will once again say
it.
Rafe. I will never learn this language. It will get but small 70
living, when it will scarce be learned till one be old.
Mariner. Nay then, farewell. And if your fortunes exceed
not your wits, you shall starve before ye sleep.   [*Exit.*]
Rafe. Was there ever such cozening? Come, let us to the
woods and see what fortune we may have before they be 75
made ships. As for our master, he is drowned.
Dick. I will this way.
Robin. I, this.
Rafe. I, this. And this day twelve-month let us all meet here
again. It may be we shall either beg together or hang 80
together.
Dick. It skills not, so we be together. But let us sing now,
though we cry hereafter.

[*Song.*

Omnes.   *Rocks, shelves, and sands and seas, farewell.*
                   Fie! who would dwell,   85
                   In such a hell
                 As is a ship which drunk does reel,
                 Taking salt healths from deck to keel?

Robin.   *Up were we swallowed in wet graves,*
Dick.   *All soused in waves,*   90

67 *dullard*] fool, dunce   82 *skills not*] does not matter   83.1 *Song*] Not found
in the Quarto. See Note on the Texts p.xxiv above.   90 *soused*] drenched

142

Rafe.	By Neptune's slaves.
Omnes.	What shall we do being tossed to shore?
Robin.	Milk some blind tavern, and there roar.

Rafe.	'Tis brave, my boys, to sail on land,
	For being well manned,	95
	We can cry, 'Stand!'
Dick.	The trade of pursing ne'er shall fail,
	· Until the hangman cries, 'Strike sail!'

Omnes.	Rove then no matter whither,
	In fair or stormy weather,	100
	And as we live, let's die together,
	One hempen caper cuts a feather.]

                                                Exeunt.

93 *milk*] exploit   93 *roar*] revel uproariously   95-6 *well manned . . . stand*] An allusion to the highwayman's traditional cry of 'stand and deliver' (i.e. we can become highway robbers), but with bawdy overtones.   97 *pursing*] taking purses, stealing   98 *strike sail*] nautical command to lower the sails, thus implying the end of a voyage (here the voyage of life)   102 *One . . . feather*] a flourish on the end of a rope will divide our unity (play on 'to cut a feather' meaning both to split hairs and to make the water foam before the bow of a ship, and on 'caper' meaning both to dance and a Dutch privateer)

Actus Secundus

SCAENA PRIMA

[Enter] GALLATHEA *alone.*

Gallathea. Blush, Gallathea, that must frame thy affection fit
for thy habit, and therefore be thought immodest because
thou art unfortunate. Thy tender years cannot dissemble
this deceit, nor thy sex bear it. Oh, would the gods had
made me as I seem to be, or that I might safely be what 5
I seem not! Thy father doteth, Gallathea, whose blind love
corrupteth his fond judgment, and, jealous of thy death,
seemeth to dote on thy beauty, whose fond care carrieth
his partial eye as far from truth as his heart is from falsehood. But why dost thou blame him, or blab what thou 10
art, when thou shouldst only counterfeit what thou art
not? But whist, here cometh a lad. I will learn of him how
to behave myself.

Enter PHILLIDA *in man's attire.*

Phillida [aside]. I neither like my gait nor my garments, the
one untoward, the other unfit; both unseemly. Oh, 15
Phillida! – But yonder stayeth one, and therefore say
nothing, but 'Oh, Phillida!'

Gallathea [aside]. I perceive that boys are in as great disliking
of themselves as maids. Therefore, though I wear the
apparel, I am glad I am not the person. 20

Phillida [aside]. It is a pretty boy and a fair. He might well
have been a woman; but because he is not, I am glad I am,
for now under the colour of my coat I shall decipher the
follies of their kind.

Gallathea [aside]. I would salute him, but I fear I should 25
make a curtsy instead of a leg.

Phillida [aside]. If I durst trust my face as well as I do my

---

1-2 *frame . . . habit*] accommodate your interests to your garments   7 *fond*] foolish, loving   7 *jealous*] apprehensive   15 *untoward*] awkward   23 *colour of my
coat*] the pretence of my masculine disguise   24 *kind*] species   26 *leg*] bow

144

habit I would spend some time to make pastime, for say
what they will of a man's wit, it is no second thing to be a
woman.   30

Gallathea [*aside*].   All the blood in my body would be in my
face if he should ask me, as the question among men is
common, 'Are you a maid?'

Phillida [*aside*].   Why stand I still? Boys should be bold. But
here cometh a brave train that will spill all our talk.   35

       Enter DIANA, TELUSA, *and* EUROTA.

Diana.   God speed, fair boy.

Gallathea.   You are deceived, lady.

Diana.   Why, are you no boy?

Gallathea.   No fair boy.

Diana.   But, I see, an unhappy boy.   40

Telusa.   Saw you not the deer come this way? He flew down
the wind, and I believe you have blanched him.

Gallathea.   Whose deer was it, lady?

Telusa.   Diana's deer.

Gallathea.   I saw none but mine own dear.   45

Telusa.   This wag is wanton or a fool. Ask the other, Diana.

Gallathea [*aside*].   I know not how it cometh to pass, but
yonder boy is in mine eye too beautiful. I pray gods the
ladies think him not their dear.

Diana [*to Phillida*].   Pretty lad, do your sheep feed in the   50
forest, or are you strayed from you[r] flock? Or on purpose come ye to mar Diana's pastime?

Phillida.   I understand not one word you speak.

Diana.   What, art thou neither lad nor shepherd?

Phillida.   My mother said I could be no lad till I was twenty   55
year old, nor keep sheep till I could tell them. And therefore, lady, neither lad nor shepherd is here.

Telusa.   These boys are both agreed; either they are very
pleasant or too perverse. You were best, lady, make them

---

35 *brave*] gallant, imposing   35 *spill*] ruin   42 *blanched him*] made him turn back
46 *wanton*] perverse   51 *you[r]*] Quarto reads 'you'. Corrected in 1632 edition.
56 *tell*] count

tusk these woods whilst we stand with our bows, and so 60
use them as beagles since they have so good mouths.

Diana.   I will. [*To Phillida.*] Follow me without delay or
excuse, and if you can do nothing, yet shall you halloo the
deer.

Phillida.   I am willing to go – [*aside*] not for these ladies' com- 65
pany, because myself am a virgin, but for that fair boy's
favour, who I think be a god.

Diana [*to Gallathea*].   You, sir boy, shall also go.

Gallathea.   I must, if you command. [*Aside.*] And would if
you had not.   70

Exeunt.

ACTUS SECUNDUS   SCAENA SECUNDA

[*Enter*] CUPID *alone, in nymph's apparel, and* NEPTUNE, *listening.*

Cupid.   Now, Cupid, under the shape of a silly girl show the
power of a mighty god. Let Diana and all her coy nymphs
know that there is no heart so chaste but thy bow can
wound, nor eyes so modest but thy brands can kindle, nor
thoughts so staid but thy shafts can make wavering, 5
weak and wanton. Cupid, though he be a child, is no baby.
I will make their pains my pastimes, and so confound
their loves in their own sex that they shall dote in their
desires, delight in their affections, and practise only
impossibilities. Whilst I truant from my mother I will use 10
some tyranny in these woods, and so shall their exercise in
foolish love be my excuse for running away. I will see
whether fair faces be always chaste, or Diana's virgins

60 *tusk*] beat   67 *favour*] pun (appearance / goodwill)
1 *silly*] weak, simple   4 *brands*] torches   5 *staid*] pun on 'staid' (sober) and
'stayed' (unwavering)

146

only modest, else will I spend both my shafts and shifts. And then, ladies, if you see these dainty dames 15 entrapped in love, say softly to yourselves, 'We may all love'.

Exit.

Neptune. Do silly shepherds go about to deceive great Neptune in putting on man's attire upon women, and Cupid, to make sport, deceive them all by using a 20 woman's apparel upon a god? Then, Neptune, that hast taken sundry shapes to obtain love, stick not to practise some deceit to show thy deity, and having often thrust thyself into the shape of beasts to deceive men, be not coy to use the shape of a shepherd to show thyself a god. 25 Neptune cannot be overreached by swains, himself is subtle; and if Diana be overtaken by craft, Cupid is wise. I will into these woods and mark all – and in the end will mar all.

Exit.

ACTUS SECUNDUS   SCAENA TERTIA

Enter RAFE *alone.*

Rafe.   Call you this seeking of fortunes, when one can find nothing but birds' nests? Would I were out of these woods, for I shall have but wooden luck. Here's nothing but the screaking of owls, croaking of frogs, hissing of adders, barking of foxes, walking of hags. But what be 5 these?

Enter FAIRIES *dancing and playing, and so exeunt.*

I will follow them. To hell I shall not go, for so fair faces never can have such hard fortunes. What black boy is this?

14 *spend . . . shifts*] exhaust both my arrows and my wiles   22 *stick not*] do not scruple
3 *wooden luck*] poor fortune (contrasting with the golden hopes Peter subsequently holds out)

147

Enter the Alchemist's boy, PETER.

Peter. What a life do I lead with my master! Nothing but
blowing of bellows, beating of spirits, and scraping of 10
crosslets! It is a very secret science, for none almost can
understand the language of it: sublimation, almigation,
calcination, rubification, incorporation, circination,
cementation, albification, and frementation, with as many
terms unpossible to be uttered as the art to be compassed. 15

Rafe [aside]. Let me cross myself! I never heard so many
great devils in a little monkey's mouth!

Peter. Then our instruments: crosslets, sublivatories, cucurbits, limbecks, descensories, vials manual and mural for
imbibing and conbibing, bellows mollificative and indu- 20
rative.

Rafe [aside]. What language is this? Do they speak so?

Peter. Then our metals – saltpeter, vitriol, sal tartar, sal
perperate, argol, resagar, sal armoniac, egrimony, lumany,
brimstone, valerian, tartar alum, breemwort, glass, 25

10 *spirits*] one of the four liquid essences defined by mediaeval alchemists
11 *crosslets*] crucibles   12 *sublimation*] turning a solid substance by heat into a
vapour, which then resolidifies on cooling   12 *almigation*] amalgamation: the
softening of metals through combining with mercury   13 *calcination*] reduction
(through heat) to powder form   13 *rubification*] the process of heating until red
13 *incorporation*] the combining of substances to form a homogenous compound
13 *circination*] revolving   14 *cementation*] combining one substance with another
at high temperature, without liquefaction   14 *albification*] whitening   14 *frementation*] fermentation   18 *sublivatories*] sublimatories, vessels used in sublimation, see II.iii.12n.   18-9 *cucurbits*] vessels used in distillation   19 *limbecks*]
distillation apparatus   19 *descensories*] apparatus for distilling downwards (i.e.
with heat applied at the top of the vessel)   19-20 *vials . . . conbibing*] hand-held
and wall-mounted vessels for moistening and mixing   20-1 *bellows . . . indurative*]
bellows for softening and hardening   23 *sal tartar*] salt of tartar   23-4 *sal perperate*] sal preparate, prepared salt   24 *argol*] tartar adhering to the cask after
fermenting wine   24 *resagar*] realgar, red powder composed of equal propor-
tions of sulphur and arsenic   24 *sal armoniac*] sal ammoniac, ammonium chlo-
ride   24 *egrimony*] agrimony, a plant with small yellow flowers   24 *lumany*]
unknown substance (possibly a plant) used in alchemy   25 *brimstone*] sulphur
25 *valerian*] strong smelling herb with small pink or white flowers   25 *tartar
alum*] bitartrate of potash (tartar), a double sulphate of aluminium and potassium
(alum)   25 *breemwort*] barm, yeast

unslaked lime, chalk, ashes, hair, and what not – to make
I know not what.

Rafe [*aside*]. My hair beginneth to stand upright! Would the
boy would make an end.

Peter. And yet such a beggarly science it is, and so strong 30
on multiplication, that the end is to have neither gold, wit,
nor honesty.

Rafe [*coming forward*]. Then am I just of thy occupation.
What, fellow, well met!

Peter. Fellow? Upon what acquaintance? 35

Rafe. Why, thou sayst the end of thy occupation is to have
neither wit, money, nor honesty, and methinks, at a blush,
thou shouldst be one of my occupation.

Peter. Thou art deceived. My master is an alchemist.

Rafe. What's that? A man? 40

Peter. A little more than a man, and a hair's breadth less
than a god. He can make of thy cap, gold, and by multiplication of one groat, three old angels. I have known him
of the tag of a point to make a silver bowl of a pint.

Rafe. That makes thee have never a point, they all be turned 45
to pots. But if he can do this, he shall be a god altogether.

Peter. If thou have any gold to work on, thou art then made
for ever. For with one pound of gold he will go near to
pave ten acres of ground.

Rafe. How might a man serve him, and learn his cunning? 50

Peter. Easily. First seem to understand the terms, and speci-
ally mark these points. In our art there are four spirits.

Rafe. Nay, I have done if you work with devils.

Peter. Thou art gross. We call those spirits that are the
grounds of our art, and (as it were) the metals more in- 55
corporative for domination. The first spirit is quicksilver.

---

26 *unslaked lime*] lime unmixed with water 31 *multiplication*] enhancing the
value of base or precious metals through an alchemical process 34 *fellow*] comrade 37 *at a blush*] at first glance 43 *groat*] silver coin worth 4d. 43 *old
angels*] gold coins bearing the device of the archangel Michael (worth 20
groats) 44 *tag of a point*] See I.iv.36-7n. 54 *gross*] thick witted, dull 55-6
incorporative for domination] capable of combining to gain predominance over
other metals

Rafe. That is my spirit, for my silver is so quick that I have
   much ado to catch it, and when I have it, it is so nimble
   that I cannot hold it. I thought there was a devil in it.
Peter. The second, orpiment.   60
Rafe. That's no spirit, but a word to conjure a spirit.
Peter. The third, sal armoniac.
Rafe. A proper word.
Peter. The fourth, brimstone.
Rafe. That's a stinking spirit. I thought there was some   65
   spirit in it, because it burnt so blue. For my mother would
   often tell me that when the candle burnt blue there was
   some ill spirit in the house, and now I perceive it was the
   spirit Brimstone.
Peter. Thou canst remember these four spirits?   70
Rafe. Let me alone to conjure them.
Peter. Now are there also seven bodies – but here cometh
   my master.
                    Enter ALCHEMIST.
Rafe. This is a beggar.
Peter. No, such cunning men must disguise themselves as   75
   though there were nothing in them, for otherwise they
   shall be compelled to work for princes, and so be con-
   strained to bewray their secrets.
Rafe. I like not his attire, but am enamoured of his art.
Alchemist [to himself]. An ounce of silver, limed, as much 80
   of crude mercury, of spirits four, being tempered with the
   bodies seven, by multiplying of it ten times, comes for one
   pound eight thousand pounds, so that I may have only
   beechen coals.
Rafe. Is it possible?   85
Peter. It is more certain than certainty.

60 *orpiment*] a yellow arsenic compound   65-6 *stinking spirit . . . blue*] A reference to the fact that brimstone smells unpleasant and burns with a blue flame. A
candle burning blue traditionally signified the presence of a spirit.   72 *seven
bodies*] the seven metals known to the ancient world (gold, silver, mercury, cop-
per, iron, tin, and lead)   78 *bewray*] reveal   84 *beechen coals*] beech-wood firing,
highly prized by alchemists for its quick burning property

150

Rafe. I'll tell thee one secret. I stole a silver thimble. Dost
thou think that he will make it a pottle pot?

Peter. A pottle pot? Nay, I dare warrant it, a whole cupboard of plate! Why, of the quintessence of a leaden plum-   90
met he hath framed twenty dozen of silver spoons. Look
how he studies! I durst venture my life he is now casting
about how of his breath he may make golden bracelets, for
oftentimes of smoke he hath made silver drops.

Rafe. What do I hear?   95

Peter. Didst thou never hear how Jupiter came in a golden
shower to Danae?

Rafe. I remember that tale.

Peter. That shower did my master make of a spoonful of
tartar-alum. But with the fire of blood and the corrosive of 100
the air, he is able to make nothing infinite – but whist, he
espieth us.

Alchemist. What, Peter, do you loiter, knowing that every
minute increaseth our mine?

Peter. I was glad to take air, for the metal came so fast that 105
I feared my face would have been turned to silver.

Alchemist. But what stripling is this?

Peter. One that is desirous to learn your craft.

Alchemist. Craft, sir boy! You must call it mystery.

Rafe. All is one. A crafty mystery and a mystical craft.   110

Alchemist. Canst thou take pains?

Rafe. Infinite.

Alchemist. But thou must be sworn to be secret, and then
I will entertain thee.

Rafe. I can swear, though I be a poor fellow, as well as the 115
best man in the shire. But, sir, I much marvel that you,
being so cunning, should be so ragged.

---

88 *pottle pot*] half gallon container   90 *plate*] silver dishes   92-3 *casting about*]
considering   96-7 *Jupiter . . . Danae*] A reference to the seduction of Danae by
Jupiter, who turned himself into a shower of gold to gain access to the tower in
which she had been confined by her father.   114 *entertain thee*] admit you to my
service

Alchemist.   O, my child, gryphes make their nests of gold
   though their coats are feathers, and we feather our nests
   with diamonds, though our garments be but frieze. If thou 120
   knewest the secret of this science, the cunning would
   make thee so proud that thou wouldst disdain the outward pomp.
Peter.   My master is so ravished with his art that we many
   times go supperless to bed, for he will make gold of his 125
   bread, and such is the drouth of his desire that we all wish
   our very guts were gold.
Rafe.   I have good fortune to light upon such a master.
Alchemist.   When in the depth of my skill I determine to try
   the uttermost of mine art, I am dissuaded by the gods. 130
   Otherwise, I durst undertake to make the fire as it flames,
   gold; the wind as it blows, silver; the water as it runs, lead;
   the earth as it stands, iron; the sky, brass; and men's
   thoughts, firm metals.
Rafe.   I must bless myself, and marvel at you.   135
Alchemist.   Come in, and thou shalt see all.   *Exit.*
Rafe.   I follow, I run, I fly! They say my father hath a golden
   thumb; you shall see me have a golden body.   *Exit.*
Peter.   I am glad of this, for now I shall have leisure to run
   away. Such a bald art as never was! Let him keep his new 140
   man, for he shall never see his old again! God shield me
   from blowing gold to nothing, with a strong imagination
   to make nothing anything!

Exit.

---

118 *gryphes*] griffins, fabulous creatures with the head and wings of an eagle and
the body of a lion   120 *frieze*] coarse woollen cloth   126 *drouth*] extreme
thirst   137-8 *father . . . thumb*] A reference to the fact that Rafe's father is a miller
(cf. 'An honest miller has a golden thumb': proverbial)   140 *bald*] paltry, unpro-
ductive

[Enter] GALLATHEA *alone.*

Gallathea.   How now, Gallathea, miserable Gallathea, that
having put on the apparel of a boy thou canst [not] also
put on the mind! Oh, fair Melebeus! Aye, too fair, and
therefore, I fear, too proud. Had it not been better for thee
to have been a sacrifice to Neptune than a slave to   5
Cupid; to die for thy country than to live in thy fancy; to
be a sacrifice than a lover? Oh, would when I hunted his
eye with my heart, he might have seen my heart with his
eyes! Why did Nature to him, a boy, give a face so fair, or
to me, a virgin, a fortune so hard? I will now use for the 10
distaff, the bow, and play at quoits abroad that was wont
to sew in my sampler at home. It may be, Gallathea –.
Foolish Gallathea, what may be? Nothing. Let me follow
him into the woods, and thou, sweet Venus, be my guide.

Exit.

Enter PHILLIDA *alone.*

Phillida.   Poor Phillida, curse the time of thy birth and rareness of thy beauty, the unaptness of thy apparel and the
untamedness of thy affections! Art thou no sooner in the
habit of a boy but thou must be enamoured of a boy? What
shalt thou do, when what best liketh thee most discon-   5
tenteth thee? Go into the woods, watch the good times,

---

2 *not*] Omitted from Quarto   3 *Melebeus*] The disguised maidens have assumed
their fathers' names   11 *distaff*] part of a hand-held spinning wheel, and thus
suggestive of occupations suitable for women (cf. *Campaspe*, I.ii.14n. above)
11 *quoits*] male sport involving throwing a disc over or near a peg
5-6 *when . . . discontenteth thee*] when what is most pleasing to you causes you
greatest unhappiness

his best moods, and transgress in love a little of thy modesty. I will! I dare not. Thou must! I cannot. Then pine in thine own peevishness. I will not. I will! Ah, Phillida, do something, nay, anything, rather than live thus. Well, what 10 I will do, myself knows not, but what I ought I know too well. And so I go resolute, either to bewray my love, or suffer shame.

Exit.

Actus Tertius

SCAENA PRIMA

[Enter] TELUSA *alone.*

Telusa.   How now? What new conceits, what strange contraries breed in thy mind? Is thy Diana become a Venus, thy chaste thoughts turned to wanton looks, thy conquering modesty to a captive imagination? Beginnest thou with piralis to die in the air and live in the fire, to leave 5 the sweet delight of hunting and to follow the hot desire of love? Oh Telusa, these words are unfit for thy sex, being a virgin, but apt for thy affections, being a lover. And can there in years so young, in education so precise, in vows so holy, and in a heart so chaste enter either a strong 10 desire, or a wish, or a wavering thought of love? Can Cupid's brands quench Vesta's flames, and his feeble shafts headed with feathers pierce deeper than Diana's arrows headed with steel? Break thy bow, Telusa, that seekest to break thy vow, and let those hands that aimed 15 to hit the wild hart scratch out those eyes that have

1 *conceits*] ideas   5 *piralis . . . fire*] winged insect thought to flourish in fire but to languish when out of it   12 *Vesta's flames*] the eternal fire burning in the temple of Vesta and tended by her virgins, emblematic of chastity

wounded thy tame heart. O vain and only naked name of chastity, that is made eternal and perisheth by time; holy, and is infected by fancy; divine, and is made mortal by folly! Virgins' hearts, I perceive, are not unlike cotton 20 trees, whose fruit is so hard in the bud that it soundeth like steel, and, being ripe, poureth forth nothing but wool; and their thoughts like the leaves of lunary, which, the further they grow from the sun, the sooner they are scorched with his beams. Oh, Melebeus, because thou art fair must I be 25 fickle, and false my vow because I see thy virtue? Fond girl that I am, to think of love: nay, vain profession that I follow to disdain love. But here cometh Eurota. I must now put on a red mask and blush, lest she perceive my pale face and laugh.   30

Enter EUROTA.

Eurota.   Telusa, Diana bid me hunt you out, and saith that you care not to hunt with her; but if you follow any other game than she hath roused, your punishment shall be to bend all our bows and weave all our strings. Why look ye so pale, so sad, so wildly?   35

Telusa.   Eurota, the game I follow is the thing I fly; my strange disease, my chief desire.

Eurota.   I am no Oedipus to expound riddles, and I muse how thou canst be Sphinx to utter them. But I pray thee, Telusa, tell me what thou ailest. If thou be sick, this 40 ground hath leaves to heal; if melancholy, here are pastimes to use; if peevish, wit must wean it, or time, or counsel. If thou be in love (for I have heard of such a beast called love) it shall be cured. Why blushest thou, Telusa?   45

Telusa.   To hear thee in reckoning my pains to recite thine

23-5 *lunary . . . beams*] moonwort, a plant that flourishes in the early spring before the heat of the summer   34 *bend . . . bows*] i.e. string them ready for hunting 38-9 *Oedipus . . . Sphinx to utter them*] Oedipus became king of Thebes by solving a riddle posed by a female monster with the body of a winged lion (the Sphinx), who was terrorizing the city by slaying all those who could not answer her question.   42 *wit must wean it*] intelligence must disengage you from it

own. I saw, Eurota, how amorously you glanced your eye
on the fair boy in the white coat, and how cunningly, now
that you would have some talk of love, you hit me in the
teeth with love.   50

Eurota. I confess that I am in love, and yet swear that I
know not what it is. I feel my thoughts unknit, mine eyes
unstayed, my heart I know not how affected (or infected),
my sleeps broken and full of dreams, my wakeness sad
and full of sighs, myself in all things unlike myself. If this 55
be love, I would it had never been devised.

Telusa. Thou hast told what I am in uttering what thyself is.
These are my passions, Eurota, my unbridled passions,
my intolerable passions, which I were as good acknowledge and crave counsel, as to deny and endure peril.   60

Eurota. How did it take you first, Telusa?

Telusa. By the eyes, my wanton eyes, which conceived the
picture of his face, and hanged it on the very strings of my
heart. Oh, fair Melebeus! Oh, fond Telusa! But how did it
take you, Eurota?   65

Eurota. By the ears, whose sweet words sunk so deep into
my head that the remembrance of his wit hath bereaved
me of my wisdom. Oh, eloquent Tyterus! Oh, credulous
Eurota! But soft, here cometh Ramia. But let her not hear
us talk. We will withdraw ourselves and hear her talk.   70

[They withdraw.]
Enter RAMIA.

Ramia. I am sent to seek others that have lost myself.

Eurota [*aside*]. You shall see Ramia hath also bitten on a love
leaf.

Ramia. Can there be no heart so chaste but love can wound,
nor vows so holy but affection can violate? Vain art thou, 75
virtue, and thou, chastity, but a byword, when you both
are subject to love, of all things the most abject. If love be
a god, why should not lovers be virtuous? Love *is* a god,
and lovers *are* virtuous!

49-50 *hit me in the teeth*] reproach me with   76 *byword*] object of scorn

Eurota [*coming forward*].   Indeed, Ramia, if lovers were not   80
virtuous, then wert thou vicious.
Ramia.   What, are you come so near me?
Telusa [*coming forward*].   I think we came near you when we
said you loved.
Eurota.   Tush, Ramia, 'tis too late to recall it; to repent it a   85
shame. Therefore, I pray thee, tell what is love?
Ramia.   If myself felt only this infection I would then take
upon me the definition, but, being incident to so many, I
dare not myself describe it. But we will all talk of that in
the woods. Diana stormeth that sending one to seek   90
another she loseth all. Servia, of all the nymphs the coyest,
loveth deadly, and exclaimeth against Diana, honoureth
Venus, detesteth Vesta, and maketh a common scorn of
virtue. Clymene, whose stately looks seemed to amaze the
greatest lords, stoopeth, yieldeth, and fawneth on the   95
strange boy in the woods. Myself (with blushing I speak
it) am thrall to that boy, that fair boy, that beautiful boy!
Telusa.   What have we here? All in love? No other food than
fancy? No, no, she shall not have the fair boy.
Eurota.   Nor you, Telusa!   100
Ramia.   Nor you, Eurota!
Telusa.   I love Melebeus, and my deserts shall be answerable
to my desires. I will forsake Diana for him. I will die for
him.
Ramia.   So saith Clymene, and she will have him. I care   105
not. My sweet Tyterus, though he seem proud, I impute it
to childishness, who, being yet scarce out of his swath
clouts, cannot understand these deep conceits. I love him!
Eurota.   So do I – and I will have him!
Telusa.   Immodest all that we are, unfortunate all that we   110
are like to be! Shall virgins begin to wrangle for love, and
become wanton in their thoughts, in their words, in their
actions? O divine love, which art therefore called divine

82-3 *near me / near you*] physically close to me / close to understanding you
91 *coyest*] most reserved   94 *amaze*] daunt, stupefy   107-8 *swath clouts*] infant
swaddling clothes

because thou over-reachest the wisest, conquerest the chastest, and dost all things both unlikely and impossible 115 because thou art love! Thou makest the bashful, impudent; the wise, fond; the chaste, wanton; and workest contraries to our reach, because thyself is beyond reason.

Eurota. Talk no more, Telusa; your words wound. Ah, would I were no woman! 120

Ramia. Would Tyterus were no boy!

Telusa. Would Telusa were nobody

Exeunt.

ACTUS TERTIUS   SCAENA SECUNDA

[*Enter*] PHILLIDA *and* GALLATHEA.

Phillida. It is pity that Nature framed you not a woman, having a face so fair, so lovely a countenance, so modest a behaviour.

Gallathea. There is a tree in Tylos whose nuts have shells like fire, and, being cracked, the kernel is but water. 5

Phillida. What a toy is it to tell me of that tree, being nothing to the purpose! I say it is pity you are not a woman.

Gallathea. I would not wish to be a woman, unless it were because thou art a man. 10

Phillida. Nay, I do not wish [thee] to be a woman, for then I should not love thee, for I have sworn never to love a woman.

Gallathea. A strange humour in so pretty a youth, and according to mine, for myself will never love a woman. 15

4-5 *Tylos . . . water*] Source of reference unknown   6 *toy*] foolish thing, idle fancy
11 *thee*] Omitted from Quarto

Phillida. It were a shame, if a maiden should be a suitor (a thing hated in that sex), that thou shouldst deny to be her servant.

Gallathea. If it be a shame in me, it can be no commendation in you, for yourself is of that mind. 20

Phillida. Suppose I were a virgin (I blush in supposing myself one), and that under the habit of a boy were the person of a maid, if I should utter my affection with sighs, manifest my sweet love by my salt tears, and prove my loyalty unspotted and my griefs intolerable, would not 25 then that fair face pity this true heart?

Gallathea. Admit that I were as you would have me suppose that you are, and that I should with entreaties, prayers, oaths, bribes, and whatever can be invented in love, desire your favour, would you not yield?˙ 30

Phillida. Tush, you come in with 'admit'.

Gallathea. And you with 'suppose'.

Phillida [*aside*]. What doubtful speeches be these! I fear me he is as I am, a maiden.

Gallathea [*aside*]. What dread riseth in my mind! I fear the 35 boy to be as I am, a maiden.

Phillida [*aside*]. Tush, it cannot be; his voice shows the conrary.

Gallathea [*aside*]. Yet I do not think it; for he would then have blushed. 40

Phillida. Have you ever a sister?

Gallathea. If I had but one, my brother must needs have two. But, I pray, have you ever a one?

Phillida. My father had but one daughter, and therefore I could have no sister. 45

Gallathea [*aside*]. Ay me! He is as I am, for his speeches be as mine are.

Phillida [*aside*]. What shall I do? Either he is subtle or my sex simple.

17-8 *deny to be her servant*] refuse to be her devoted follower   33 *doubtful*] ambivalent

Gallathea [*aside*].   I have known divers of Diana's nymphs 50
enamoured of him, yet hath he rejected all, either as too
proud, to disdain; or too childish, not to understand; or for
that he knoweth himself to be a virgin.

Phillida [*aside*].   I am in a quandary! Diana's nymphs have
followed him and he despised them, either knowing too 55
well the beauty of his own face, or that himself is of the
same mould. I will once again try him. [*To* GALLATHEA.]
You promised me in the woods that you would love me
before all Diana's nymphs.

Gallathea.   Aye, so you would love me before all Diana's 60
nymphs.

Phillida.   Can you prefer a fond boy as I am before so fair
ladies as they are?

Gallathea.   Why should not I as well as you?

Phillida.   Come, let us into the grove and make much one of 65
another, that cannot tell what to think one of another.

Exeunt.

ACTUS TERTIUS   SCAENA TERTIA

[*Enter*] ALCHEMIST, RAFE.

Alchemist.   Rafe, my boy is run away. I trust thou wilt not
run after.

Rafe.   I would I had a pair of wings, that I might fly after.

Alchemist.   My boy was the veriest thief, the arrantest liar,
and the vilest swearer in the world; otherwise the best boy 5
in the world. He hath stolen my apparel, all my
money, and forgot nothing but to bid me farewell.

Rafe.   That will not I forget. Farewell, master!

Alchemist.   Why, thou hast not yet seen the end of my art.

Rafe.   I would I had not known the beginning. Did not 10
you promise me of my silver thimble to make a whole
cupboard of plate, and that of a Spanish needle you would
build a silver steeple?

12 *Spanish needle*] needles were largely imported in the sixteenth century

160

Alchemist. Aye, Rafe, the fortune of this art consisteth in the
measure of the fire, for if there be a coal too much or a 15
spark too little, if it be a little too hot or a thought too
soft, all our labour is in vain. Besides, they that blow must
beat time with their breaths, as musicians do with their
breasts, so as there must be of the metals, the fire, and
workers a very harmony. 20
Rafe. Nay, if you must weigh your fire by ounces, and take
measure of a man's blast, you may then make of a dram of
wind a wedge of gold, and of the shadow of one shilling
make another, so as you have an organist to tune your
temperatures. 25
Alchemist. So is it, and often doth it happen that the just
proportion of the fire and all things concur.
Rafe. Concur? Condog! I will away.
Alchemist. Then away.

Exit ALCHEMIST.

Enter ASTRONOMER [abstracted].

Rafe. An art, quoth you, that one multiplieth so much all 30
day that he wanteth money to buy meat at night! But
what have we yonder? What devout man? He will never
speak till he be urged. I will salute him. [*To the* ASTRO-
NOMER.] Sir, there lieth a purse under your feet. If I
thought it were not yours, I would take it up. 35
Astronomer. Dost thou not know that I was calculating the
nativity of Alexander's great horse?
Rafe. Why, what are you?
Astronomer. An astronomer.
Rafe. What, one of those that makes almanacs? 40
Astronomer. Ipsissimus. I can tell the minute of thy birth, the
moment of thy death, and the manner. I can tell thee what

19 *breasts*] voices (in singing)   22 *blast*] breath   22 *dram*] measure of weight
(sixty grams or one eighth of an ounce)   28 *condog*] play on the second syllable
of 'concur'   31 *meat*] food   36-7 *calculating the nativity*] working out the horo-
scope   37 *Alexander's great horse*] Bucephalus, much loved by his master (cf.
Campaspe, III.iv.35n. above)   40 *almanacs*] popular calendars (published annual-
ly) listing the months and the days and including a wealth of related astronomical and astrological data   41 *Ipsissimus*] the very same

weather shall be between this and *octogessimus octavus mirabilis annus*. When I list, I can set a trap for the sun, catch the moon with lime twigs, and go a-batfowling for 45 stars. I can tell thee things past and things to come, and with my cunning measure how many yards of clouds are beneath the sky. Nothing can happen which I foresee not: nothing shall.

Rafe. I hope, sir, you are no more than a god? 50

Astronomer. I can bring the twelve signs out of their zodiacs, and hang them up at taverns.

Rafe. I pray you, sir, tell me what you cannot do, for I perceive there is nothing so easy for you to compass as impossibilities. But what be those signs? 55

Astronomer. As a man should say, signs which govern the body. The Ram governeth the head.

Rafe. That is the worst sign for the head.

Astronomer. Why?

Rafe. Because it is the sign of an ill ewe. 60

Astronomer. Tush, that sign must be there. Then the bull for the throat, Capricornus for the knees.

Rafe. I will hear no more signs, if they be all such desperate signs. But seeing you are – I know not who to term you – shall I serve you? I would fain serve. 65

Astronomer. I accept thee.

Rafe. Happy am I, for now shall I reach thoughts, and tell how many drops of water goes to the greatest shower of rain. You shall see me catch the moon in the clips like a cony in a pursenet. 70

43-4 *octogessimus octavus mirabilis annus*] the wonderful year eighty-eight (i.e. 1588) 45 *lime twigs*] Liming twigs was a common method of catching small birds. 45 *batfowling*] catching birds at night by dazzling them with lights 51-2 *twelve . . . taverns*] a reference to the fact that many taverns were named after celestial bodies (e.g. the Seven Stars) 56-7 *signs which govern the body*] It was thought that each of the twelve signs of the zodiac exerted an influence upon a particular part of the human anatomy. 60 *an ill ewe*] a misbehaving wife (a reference to the horns of the cuckold 69 *clips*] pun on 'eclipse' and 'clip' or 'clippers' (i.e. pincers) 70 *cony*] rabbit 70 *pursenet*] bag-shaped net, the neck drawn in with a cord, used for catching small game

Astronomer. I will teach thee the golden number, the epact
and the prime.

Rafe. I will meddle no more with numbering of gold, for
multiplication is a miserable action. I pray, sir, what
weather shall we have this hour three-score year?   75

Astronomer. That I must cast by our judicials astronomical.
Therefore come in with me, and thou shall see every wrinkle of my astrological wisdom, and I will make the heavens as plain to thee as the highway. Thy cunning shall sit
cheek-by-jowl with the sun's chariot. Then shalt thou see   80
what a base thing it is to have others' thoughts creep on
the ground, whenas thine shall be stitched to the stars.

Rafe. Then I shall be translated from this mortality?

Astronomer. Thy thoughts shall be metamorphosed, and
made hail-fellows with the gods.   85

Rafe. Oh Fortune! I feel my very brains moralized, and, as
it were a certain contempt of earthly actions is crept into
my mind, by an ethereal contemplation. Come, let us in!

                                                   Exeunt.

71 *golden number*] number of any year in the lunar cycle of nineteen years (at the
close of which the moon returns to the same apparent position in relation to the
sun to the point at which it started)   71 *epact*] age of the moon (in days) on the
first day of the year (also the difference in length between the solar and lunar
years)   72 *prime*] the beginning of any period or cycle (specifically the first
appearance of the new moon)   76 *judicials astronomical*] system of concluding
the course of future events by reference to the disposition of heavenly bodies
77-8 *wrinkle*] pun (detail / trick)

163

[Enter] DIANA, TELUSA, EUROTA, RAMIA, LARISSA.

Diana. What news have we here, ladies? Are all in love?
Are Diana's nymphs become Venus' wantons? Is it a
shame to be chaste because you be amiable, or must you
needs be amorous because you are fair? Oh Venus, if this
be thy spite I will requite it with more than hate. Well   5
shalt thou know what it is to drib thine arrows up and
down Diana's leas. There is an unknown nymph that
straggleth up and down these woods, which I suspect
hath been the weaver of these woes. I saw her slumbering
by the brook side. Go search her, and bring her. If you find   10
upon her shoulder a burn, it is Cupid; if any print on her
back like a leaf, it is Medea; if any picture on her left breast
like a bird, it is Calypso. Whoever it be, bring her hither;
and speedily bring her hither.

Telusa. I will go with speed.   15

Diana. Go you, Larissa, and help her.

Larissa. I obey.   *[Exeunt* TELUSA *and* LARISSA.*]*

Diana. Now, ladies, doth not that make your cheeks blush
that makes mine ears glow; or can you remember that
without sobs which Diana cannot think on without sighs?   20
What greater dishonour could happen to Diana, or, to her
nymphs, shame, than that there can be any time so idle
that should make their heads so addle? Your chaste hearts,
my nymphs, should resemble the onyx, which is hottest
when it is whitest, and your thoughts, the more they are   25
assaulted with desires, the less they should be affected.

---

6 *drib thine arrows*] loose your shafts short or wide of the mark   7 *leas*] meadows
10-11 *If you find . . . Cupid*] a reference to the scar caused by a drop of hot oil
falling from Psyche's lamp when she rose in the night to view her lover   11-12 *if
any print . . . Medea*] Medea was noted for her knowledge of herbs   12-13 *if any
picture . . . Calypso*] Calypso fell in love with Odysseus and promised him immor-
tality if he would remain with her on her island. Odysseus, however, refused. The
bird on her shoulder appears to be Lyly's invention.   23 *addle*] confused

You should think love like Homer's moly, a white leaf and a black root, a fair show and a bitter taste. Of all trees the cedar is greatest, and hath the smallest seeds; of all affections love hath the greatest name, and the least virtue. 30 Shall it be said, and shall Venus say it – nay, shall it be seen, and shall wantons see it – that Diana, the goddess of chastity, whose thoughts are always answerable to her vows, whose eyes never glanced on desire, and whose heart abateth the point of Cupid's arrows, shall have her 35 virgins to become unchaste in desires, immoderate in affection, untemperate in love, in foolish love, in base love? Eagles cast their evil feathers in the sun, but you cast your best desires upon a shadow. The birds Ibes lose their sweetness when they lose their sights, and virgins all their 40 virtues with their unchaste thoughts – 'unchaste' Diana calleth that that hath either any show or suspicion of lightness. Oh, my dear nymphs, if you knew how loving thoughts stain lovely faces, you would be as careful to have the one as unspotted as the other beautiful! 45

Cast before your eyes the loves of Venus' trulls, their fortunes, their fancies, their ends. What are they else but Silenus' pictures – without, lambs and doves; within, apes and owls – who, like Ixion, embrace clouds for Juno, the shadows of virtue instead of the substance. The eagle's 50 feathers consume the feathers of all others, and love's

27-8 *moly . . . taste*] fabulous plant with white flowers and a black root, said by Homer to have been given by Hermes to Odysseus as a charm against the sorceress, Circe   35 *abateth*] blunts   38 *Eagles . . . sun*] Popular belief (recorded by Pliny) that eagles moisten their feathers in water, fly high into the sky to heat themselves (and open their pores) and then plummet down into water again where their feathers are renewed   39-40 *Ibes . . . sights*] The reference is to the Ibis, but the source of the allusion is not known.   48 *Silenus' pictures*] See *Campaspe*, The Prologue at the Court, line 3 in which a reference to Silenus prompts an image of pictures with an attractive exterior concealing an inner ugliness. Lancashire notes that in ancient Athens, pictures of the ugly Silenus could be 'opened to reveal images of the gods within' and that Lyly reverses this idea (*Gallathea*, III.iv.46n).   49 *Ixion . . . Juno*] Ixion attempted to seduce Juno but embraced a phantom created by Jupiter in her place, and was punished by being chained to a perpetually turning wheel.   50-1 *eagle's feathers. . . others*] See above, p.25n.

desire corrupteth all other virtues. I blush, ladies, that you having been heretofore patient of labours, should now become prentices to idleness, and use the pen for sonnets, not the needle for samplers. And how is your love placed? 55 Upon pelting boys, perhaps base of birth, without doubt weak of discretion. Aye, but they are fair! Oh, ladies, do your eyes begin to love colours, whose hearts was wont to loath them? Is Diana's chase become Venus' court, and are your holy vows turned to hollow thoughts? 60

Ramia. Madam, if love were not a thing beyond reason, we might then give a reason of our doings, but so divine is his force that it worketh effects as contrary to that we wish as unreasonable against that we ought.

Eurota. Lady, so unacquainted are the passions of love that 65 we can neither describe them nor bear them.

Diana. Foolish girls! How willing you are to follow that which you should fly. But here cometh Telusa.

Enter TELUSA *and other* [LARISSA] *with* CUPID.

Telusa. We have brought the disguised nymph, and have found on his shoulder Psyche's burn, and he confesseth 70 himself to be Cupid.

Diana. How now, sir, are you caught? Are you Cupid?

Cupid. Thou shalt see, Diana, that I dare confess myself to be Cupid.

Diana. And thou shalt see, Cupid, that I will show myself 75 to be Diana, that is, conqueror of thy loose and untamed appetites. Did thy mother, Venus, under the colour of a nymph send thee hither to wound my nymphs? Doth she add craft to her malice, and, mistrusting her deity, practise deceit? Is there no place but my groves, no per- 80 sons but my nymphs? Cruel and unkind Venus, that spiteth only chastity, thou shalt see that Diana's power shall revenge thy policy, and tame this pride. As for thee, Cupid, I will break thy bow and burn thine arrows, bind thy hands, clip thy wings, and fetter thy feet. Thou that 85

56 *pelting*] paltry   58 *love colours*] be fond of attractive / false appearances
65 *Eurota*] Quarto reads 'Larissa'

fattest others with hopes shalt be fed thyself with wishes, and thou that bindest others with golden thoughts shalt be bound thyself with golden fetters. Venus' rods are made of roses, Diana's of briars. Let Venus, that great goddess, ransom Cupid, that little god. These ladies here, 90 whom thou hast infected with foolish love, shall both tread on thee and triumph over thee. Thine own arrow shall be shot into thine own bosom, and thou shalt be enamoured not on Psyches, but on Circes. I will teach thee what it is to displease Diana, distress her nymphs, or 95 disturb her game.

Cupid. Diana, what I have done cannot be undone, but what you mean to do, shall. Venus hath some gods to her friends. Cupid shall have all!

Diana. Are you prating? I will bridle thy tongue and thy 100 power, and in spite of mine own thoughts I will set thee a task every day, which if thou finish not thou shalt feel the smart. Thou shalt be used as Diana's slave, not Venus' son. All the world shall see that I will use thee like a captive, and show myself a conqueror. Come, have him in, that we 105 may devise apt punishments for his proud presumptions.

Eurota. We will plague ye for a little god.

Telusa. We will never pity thee, though thou be a god.

Ramia. Nor I.

Larissa. Nor I. 110

Exeunt.

---

94 *Psyches . . . Circes*] Psyche epitomizes devoted love through the suffering she endured for Cupid, Circe demeaning enchantment through her effect on the followers of Odysseus (turned by her into swine). 96 *her game*] both 'her sport' and 'the animals she pursues' 100 *prating*] chattering boastfully

Actus Quartus

SCAENA PRIMA

[*Enter*] AUGUR, MELEBEUS, TYTERUS, POPULUS.

Augur. This is the day wherein you must satisfy Neptune
and save yourselves. Call together your fair daughters,
and for a sacrifice take the fairest, for better it is to offer a
virgin than suffer ruin. If you think it against Nature to
sacrifice your children, think it also against sense to 5
destroy your country. If you imagine Neptune pitiless to
desire such a prey, confess yourselves perverse to deserve
such a punishment. You see this tree, this fatal tree, whose
leaves, though they glister like gold, yet it threateneth to
fair virgins grief? To this tree must the beautifullest be 10
bound until the monster, *Agar*, carry her away, and if the
monster come not, then assure yourselves that the fairest
is concealed, and then your country shall be destroyed.
Therefore consult with yourselves, not as fathers of children, but as favourers of your country. Let Neptune have 15
his right, if you will have your quiet. Thus have I warned
you to be careful, and would wish you to be wise, knowing that whoso hath the fairest daughter hath the greatest
fortune, in losing one to save all. And so I depart to provide ceremonies for the sacrifice, and command you to 20
bring the sacrifice. *Exit* AUGUR.

Melebeus. They say, Tyterus, that you have a fair daughter.
If it be so, dissemble not, for you shall be a fortunate
father. It is a thing holy to preserve one's country, and
honourable to be the cause. 25

Tyterus. Indeed, Melebeus, I have heard you boast that you
had a fair daughter, than the which none was more beautiful. I hope you are not so careful of a child that you will
be careless of your country, or add so much to Nature that
you will detract from wisdom. 30

Melebeus. I must confess that I had a daughter, and I know
you have, but, alas, my child's cradle was her grave, and

29 *be careless of*] lack regard for

168

her swath-clout her winding sheet. I would she had lived
till now, she should willingly have died now; for what
could have happened to poor Melebeus more comfort- 35
able than to be the father of a fair child and sweet country?
Tyterus. Oh, Melebeus, dissemble you may with men,
deceive the gods you cannot. Did not I see, and very lately
see, your daughter in your arms, whenas you gave her
infinite kisses, with affection (I fear me) more than 40
fatherly? You have conveyed her away that you might cast
us all away, bereaving her the honour of her beauty and us
the benefit, preferring a common inconvenience before a
private mischief.
Melebeus. It is a bad cloth, Tyterus, that will take no colour, 45
and a simple father that can use no cunning. You make the
people believe that you wish well, when you practise
nothing but ill, wishing to be thought religious towards
the gods when I know you deceitful towards men. You
cannot overreach me, Tyterus; overshoot yourself you 50
may. It is a wily mouse that will breed in the cat's ear, and
he must halt cunningly that will deceive a cripple. Did
you ever see me kiss my daughter? You are deceived; it
was my wife. And if you thought so young a piece unfit for
so old a person, and therefore imagined it to be my 55
child, not my spouse, you must know that silver hairs
delight in golden locks, and the old fancies crave young
nurses, and frosty years must be thawed by youthful fires.
But this matter set aside, you have a fair daughter,
Tyterus, and it is pity you are so fond a father.   60
[1] Populus. You are both either too fond or too froward; for
whilst you dispute to save your daughters, we neglect to
prevent our destruction.
Alter. Come, let us away and seek out a sacrifice. We must
sift out their cunning, and let them shift for themselves. 65
                                                  Exeunt.

---

44 *mischief*] trouble, affliction   61 *[1] Populus*] Quarto reads '*Populus*'   65 *sift
out their cunning / shift for themselves*] look closely into their craftiness / manage
for themselves (with a play on 'shift', a stratagem or trick)

CUPID, TELUSA, EUROTA, LARISSA *enter, [all but* CUPID] *singing,*
[with RAMIA].

[*Telusa.*	*Oyez, oyez, if any maid*
	Whom leering Cupid has betray'd
	To frowns of spite, to eyes of scorn,
	And would in madness now see torn –
All 3.	*The boy in pieces let her come* 5
	Hither, and lay on him her doom.
Eurota.	*Oyez, oyez, has any lost*
	A heart which many a sigh hath cost,
	Is any cozen'd of a tear,
	Which, as a pearl, Disdain does wear? 10
All 3.	*Here stands the thief, let her but come*
	Hither, and lay on him her doom.
Larissa.	*Is anyone undone by fire,*
	And turn'd to ashes through desire?
	Did ever any lady weep, 15
	Being cheated of her golden sleep –
All 3.	*Stol'n by sick thoughts? The pirate's found,*
	And in her tears he shall be drown'd.
	Read his indictment, let him hear
	What he's to trust to. Boy, give ear!] 20

Telusa.   Come, Cupid, to your task. First you must undo all
these lovers' knots, because you tied them.
Cupid.   If they be true love knots, 'tis unpossible to unknit
them; if false, I never tied them.
Eurota.   Make no excuse, but to it.   25
Cupid.   Love knots are tied with eyes, and cannot be undone

1-20 *Telusa . . . give ear*] Omitted from Quarto   1 *Oyez*] cry of a town crier or
court official heralding a public announcement (cf. *Campaspe*, III.ii.56, above)
2 *leering*] both 'sidelong glancing' (with lascivious overtones) and 'beguiling'
6 *doom*] judgement

with hands; made fast with thoughts, and cannot be
unloosed with fingers. Had Diana no task to set Cupid to
but things impossible? [*They make threatening gestures.*] I
will to it.   30
Ramia.   Why, how now? You tie the knots faster!
Cupid.   I cannot choose. It goeth against my mind to make
them loose.
Eurota.   Let me see. Now 'tis unpossible to be undone.
Cupid.   It is the true love knot of a woman's heart, therefore 35
cannot be undone.
Ramia.   That falls in sunder of itself.
Cupid.   It was made of a man's thought, which will never
hang together.
Larissa.   You have undone that well.   40
Cupid.   Aye, because it was never tied well.
Telusa.   To the rest, for she will give you no rest. These two
knots are finely untied.
Cupid.   It was because I never tied them. The one was knit
by Pluto, not Cupid, by money, not love; the other by 45
force, not faith, by appointment, not affection.
Ramia.   Why do you lay that knot aside?
Cupid.   For death.
Telusa.   Why?
Cupid.   Because the knot was knit by faith, and must only 50
be unknit of death.
Eurota.   Why laugh you?
Cupid.   Because it is the fairest and the falsest, done with
greatest art and least truth, with best colours and worst
conceits.   55
Telusa.   Who tied it?
Cupid.   A man's tongue.
Larissa.   Why do you put that in my bosom.
Cupid.   Because it is only for a woman's bosom.
Larissa.   Why, what is it?   60
Cupid.   A woman's heart.

45 *Pluto*] god of the lower world, and giver of wealth   46 *appointment*] arrangement, contract

171

Telusa.   Come, let us go in and tell that Cupid hath done his
   task. Stay you behind, Larissa, and see he sleep not, for
   love will be idle; and take heed you surfeit not, for love
   will be wanton.   65

                    Exit TELUSA [*with* RAMIA *and* EUROTA].
Larissa.   Let me alone, I will find him somewhat to do.
Cupid.   Lady, can you for pity see Cupid thus punished?
Larissa.   Why did Cupid punish us without pity?
Cupid.   Is love a punishment?
Larissa.   It is no pastime.   70
Cupid.   Oh, Venus, if thou saw sawest Cupid as a captive,
   bound to obey that was wont to command, fearing ladies'
   threats that once pierced their hearts, I cannot tell whether
   thou wouldst revenge it for despite or laugh at it for disport. The time may come, Diana, and the time shall come,   75
   that thou that settest Cupid to undo knots shall entreat
   Cupid to tie knots, and you ladies that with solace have
   beheld my pains shall with sighs entreat my pity.

                    He offereth to sleep.
Larissa.   How now, Cupid, begin you to nod?

                    [*Enter* RAMIA *and* TELUSA.]
Ramia.   Come, Cupid, Diana hath devised new labours for   80
   you that are god of loves. You shall weave samplers all
   night, and lackey after Diana all day. You shall shortly
   shoot at beasts for men, because you have made beasts of
   men, and wait on ladies' trains, because thou entrappest
   ladies by trains. All the stories that are in Diana's arras   85
   which are of love you must pick out with your needle, and
   in that place sew Vesta with her nuns and Diana with her
   nymphs. How like you this, Cupid?
Cupid.   I say I will prick as well with my needle as ever I
   did with mine arrows.   90

---

74 *for despite*] in indignation (from offended pride)   74-5 *for disport*] for amuse-
ment   77 *solace*] pleasure   82 *lackey after*] dance attendance upon   83-4 *beasts
for men / made beasts of men*] animals instead of men / turned men into animals   85 *by trains*] through wiles   85 *arras*] tapestry used as a wallhanging

172

Telusa.   Diana cannot yield; she conquers affection.
Cupid.   Diana shall yield; she cannot conquer destiny.
Larissa.   Come, Cupid, you must to your business.
Cupid.   You shall find me so busy in your heads that you
   shall wish I had been idle with your hearts.   95

                                                     Exeunt.

ACTUS QUARTUS   SCAENA TERTIA

[Enter] NEPTUNE *alone.*
Neptune.   This day is the solemn sacrifice at this tree, wherein the fairest virgin (were not the inhabitants faithless)
   should be offered unto me, but so overcareful are fathers
   to their children that they forget the safety of their country,
   and, fearing to become unnatural, become unreasonable.   5
   Their sleights may blear men; deceive me they cannot. I
   will be here at the hour, and show as great cruelty as they
   have done craft; and well shall they know that Neptune
   should have been entreated, not cozened.

                                                         Exit.

6 *blear*] make dim-sighted (i.e. deceive)

173

Enter GALLATHEA *and* PHILLIDA.

Phillida. I marvel what virgin the people will present. It is happy you are none, for then it would have fallen to your lot because you are so fair.

Gallathea. If you had been a maiden too, I need not to have feared, because you are fairer.   5

Phillida. I pray thee, sweet boy, flatter not me, speak truth of thyself, for in mine eye of all the world thou art fairest.

Gallathea. These be fair words, but far from thy true thoughts. I know mine own face in a true glass, and desire not to see it in a flattering mouth.   10

Phillida. Oh, would I did flatter thee, and that fortune would not flatter me. I love thee as a brother, but love not me so!

Gallathea. No, I will not, but love thee better, because I cannot love as a brother.   15

Phillida. Seeing we are both boys, and both lovers, that our affection may have some show, and seem as it were love, let me call thee mistress.

Gallathea. I accept that name, for divers before have called me mistress.   20

Phillida. For what cause?

Gallathea. Nay, there lie the myst'ries.

Phillida. Will not you be at the sacrifice?

Gallathea. No.

Phillida. Why?   25

Gallathea. Because I dreamt that if I were there I should be turned to a virgin, and then, being so fair (as thou sayst I am), I should be offered (as thou knowest one must). But will not you be there?

11-12 *flatter / flatter*] overpraise / inspire with unfounded hope   18-22 *mistress / mistress / myst'ries*] object of courtship / courtesy title used to a woman / plural of mystery (the final pun obscured by modern spelling. Quarto reads 'mistris'. 'mistris', 'mistrisse')

Phillida.   Not unless I were sure that a boy might be sacri- 30
ficed, and not a maiden.
Gallathea.   Why, then you are in danger.
Phillida.   But I would escape it by deceit. But seeing we are
resolved to be both absent, let us wander into these groves
till the hour be past.   35
Gallathea.   I am agreed, for then my fear will be past.
Phillida.   Why, what dost thou fear?
Gallathea.   Nothing, but that you love me not.   *Exit.*
Phillida.   I will. Poor Phillida, what shouldst thou think of
thyself, that lovest one that, I fear me, is as thyself is? 40
And may it not be that her father practised the same deceit
with her that my father hath with me, and, knowing her to
be fair, feared she should be unfortunate? If it be so,
Phillida, how desperate is thy case! If it be not, how doubtful! For if she be a maiden, there is no hope of my love; if 45
a boy, a hazard. I will after him or her, and lead a melancholy life, that look for a miserable death.
                                                        Exit.

Actus Quintus

Enter RAFE *alone.*

Rafe. No more masters now, but a mistress, if I can light on her. An astronomer – ! Of all occupations that's the worst. Yet well fare the Alchemist, for he keeps good fires though he gets no gold. The other stands warming himself by staring on the stars, which I think he can as soon number 5 as know their virtues. He told me a long tale of *octogessimus octavus* and the meeting of the conjunctions and planets, and in the meantime he fell backward himself into a pond. I asked him why he foresaw not that by the stars; he said he knew it, but contemned it. But soft, is not this 10 my brother, Robin?

Enter ROBIN.

Robin. Yes, as sure as thou art Rafe.

Rafe. What, Robin! What news? What fortune?

Robin. Faith, I have had but bad fortune. But, I prithee, tell me thine. 15

Rafe. I have had two masters, not by art, but by nature. One said that by multiplying he would make of a penny ten pound.

Robin. Aye, but could he do it?

Rafe. Could he do it, quoth you? Why, man, I saw a pretty 20 wench come to his shop, where with puffing, blowing and sweating he so plied her that he multiplied her.

Robin. How?

Rafe. Why, he made her of one, two.

Robin. What, by fire? 25

Rafe. No, by the philosopher's stone.

---

1 *mistress*] female employer (with bawdy implications of 'sexual partner') 1-2 *light on her*] find one (with bawdy implications of 'descend onto') 3 *well fare*] good luck to 10 *contemned*] despised 26 *philosopher's stone*] the solid substance sought through alchemy and reputed to turn base metals into gold (here with a pun on 'stone', i.e. testicle)

Robin.   Why, have philosophers such stones?
Rafe.   Aye, but they lie in a privy cupboard.
Robin.   Why, then, thou art rich if thou have learned this
cunning.   30
Rafe.   Tush, this was nothing! He would of a little fasting
spittle make a hose and doublet of cloth of silver.
Robin.   Would I had been with him, for I have had almost no
meat but spittle since I came to the woods.
Rafe.   How, then, didst thou live?   35
Robin.   Why, man, I served a fortune-teller, who said I
should live to see my father hanged and both my brothers
beg. So I conclude the mill shall be mine, and I live by
imagination still.
Rafe.   Thy master was an ass, and looked on the lines of thy   40
hands, but my other master was an astronomer, which
could pick my nativity out of the stars. I should have half
a dozen stars in my pocket if I have not lost them. But here
they be. – Sol, Saturn, Jupiter, Mars, Venus –.
Robin.   Why, these be but names!   45
Rafe.   Aye, but by these he gathereth that I was a Jovialist,
born of a Thursday, and that I should be a brave Venerean,
and get all my good luck on a Friday.
Robin.   'Tis strange that a fish day should be a flesh day.
Rafe.   O Robin, *Venus orta mari*, Venus was born of the sea,   50
the sea will have fish, fish must have wine, wine will have
flesh, for *caro carnis genus est muliebre*. But soft, here
cometh that notable villain that once preferred me to the
Alchemist.

Enter PETER.

---

32 *cloth of silver*] textile composed of silver threads interwoven with silk or
wool   32 and 34 *spittle / spittle*] saliva / frothy secretion of insects found on certain
plants (cf. cuckoo spit)   46-8 *Jovialist . . . Friday*] An allusion to the fact that the
days of the week were thought to be governed by the planets. Rafe is jovial in that
he is born on Thursday, governed by Jupiter (i.e. Jove), and, being given to ven-
ery, is lucky on Fridays (governed by Venus).   49 *fish day . . . flesh day*] An allusion to the Christian practice of eating fish (rather than meat) on Fridays. The pun
is on flesh as 'meat' and as 'indulgence in fleshly pursuits'.   52 *caro . . .
muliebre*] *caro carnis* [flesh] is feminine in gender   53 *preferred*] recommended

Peter. So I had a master, I would not care what became of 55
me.

Rafe [aside to ROBIN]. Robin, thou shalt see me fit him. [*More
loudly.*] So I had a servant, I care neither for his conditions,
his qualities, nor his person.

Peter. What, Rafe? Well met! No doubt you had a warm 60
service of my master, the Alchemist?

Rafe. 'Twas warm indeed, for the fire had almost burnt out
mine eyes, and yet my teeth still watered with hunger, so
that my service was both too hot and too cold. I melted all
my meat, and made only my slumber thoughts, and so 65
had a full head and an empty belly. But where hast thou
been since?

Peter. With a brother of thine, I think, for he hath such a
coat, and two brothers, as he saith, seeking of fortunes.

Robin. 'Tis my brother Dick! I prithee, let's go to him. 70

Rafe. Sirrah, what was he doing that he came not with thee?

Peter. He hath gotten a master, now, that will teach him to
make you both his younger brothers.

Rafe. Aye, thou passest for devising impossibilities! That's
as true as thy master could make silver pots of tags of 75
points.

Peter. Nay, he will teach him to cozen you both, and so get
the mill to himself.

Rafe. Nay, if he be both our cousins, I will be his great-
grandfather and Robin shall be his uncle. But I pray thee, 80
bring us to him quickly, for I am great-bellied with conceit
till I see him.

---

57 *fit him*] punish him in an appropriate way 58 *conditions*] moral character,
social circumstances 65 *made only . . . thoughts*] created only dreams 73 *younger
brothers*] Dick is the youngest of the three brothers and Rafe the eldest (implied in
lines 79-80 below). 74 *passest*] excel 77 *cozen*] cheat 77-8 *get the mill to himself*] By the laws of inheritance obtaining during the period, Dick could inherit the
mill legally only if both Rafe and Robin pre-deceased him. 79-80 *if he be . . .
uncle*] pun on 'cozen' (Quarto reading at both lines 77 and 79) signifying both 'to
cheat' and 'a kinsman' (i.e. 'even if he is kinsman to and cheat both of us, we will
still be before him in both respects') 81 *great-bellied with conceit*] pregnant with
the thought

178

Peter.   Come, then, and go with me, and I will bring ye to
him straight.

Exeunt.

ACTUS QUINTUS   SCAENA SECUNDA

[Enter] AUGUR, ERICTHINIS.

Augur.   Bring forth the virgin, the fatal virgin, the fairest
virgin, if you mean to appease Neptune and preserve your
country.

Ericthinis.   Here she cometh, accompanied only with men,
because it is a sight unseemly (as all virgins say) to see   5
the misfortune of a maiden, and terrible to behold the
fierceness of *Agar*, that monster.

Enter HEBE, *with other[s] to the sacrifice.*

Hebe.   Miserable and accursed Hebe, that being neither fair
nor fortunate, thou shouldst be thought most happy and
beautiful. Curse thy birth, thy life, thy death, being born   10
to live in danger, and, having lived, to die by deceit. Art
thou the sacrifice to appease Neptune and satisfy the custom, the bloody custom, ordained for the safety of thy
country? Aye, Hebe, poor Hebe, men will have it so,
whose forces command our weak natures: nay, the gods   15
will have it so, whose powers dally with our purposes.
The Egyptians never cut their dates from the tree, because
they are so fresh and green; it is thought wickedness to
pull roses from the stalks in the garden of Palestine, for
that they have so lively a red; and whoso cutteth the   20
incense tree in Arabia before it fall, committeth sacrilege.
Shall it only be lawful amongst us in the prime of youth
and pride of beauty to destroy both youth and beauty, and

84 *straight*] immediately
7.1 *other[s]*] Quarto reads *'other'* but Ericthinis states that Hebe is accompanied
by 'men' (see line 4 above).   9 *happy*] fortunate

179

what was honoured in fruits and flowers as a virtue, to
violate in a virgin as a vice?   25
   But, alas, destiny alloweth no dispute. Die, Hebe! Hebe
die! Woeful Hebe, and only accursed Hebe! Farewell the
sweet delights of life, and welcome now the bitter pangs
of death. Farewell you chaste virgins, whose thoughts are
divine, whose faces fair, whose fortunes are agreeable to 30
your affections. Enjoy, and long enjoy, the pleasure of your
curled locks, the amiableness of your wished looks, the
sweetness of your tuned voices, the content of your
inward thoughts, the pomp of your outward shows. Only
Hebe biddeth farewell to all the joys that she conceived   35
and you hope for, that she possessed and you shall.
Farewell the pomp of princes' courts, whose roofs are
embossed with gold and whose pavements are decked
with fair ladies; where the days are spent in sweet
delights, the nights in pleasant dreams; where chastity   40
honoureth affections and commandeth, yieldeth to desire
and conquereth. Farewell the sovereign of all virtue and
goddess of all virgins, Diana, whose perfections are
impossible to be numbered and therefore infinite, never to
be matched and therefore immortal. Farewell sweet par-   45
ents, yet, to be mine, unfortunate parents. How blessed
had you been in barrenness; how happy had I been if I had
not been! Farewell life, vain life, wretched life, whose sor-
rows are long, whose end doubtful, whose miseries certain, whose hopes innumerable, whose fears intolerable.   50
Come, death, and welcome, death, whom nature cannot
resist because necessity ruleth, nor defer because destiny
hasteth. Come, *Agar*, thou unsatiable monster of maidens'
blood and devourer of beauties' bowels, glut thyself till
thou surfeit, and let my life end thine. Tear these tender 55
joints with thy greedy jaws, these yellow locks with thy
black feet, this fair face with thy foul teeth. Why abatest
thou thy wonted swiftness? I am fair, I am a virgin, I am
ready. Come, *Agar*, thou horrible monster, and farewell
world, thou viler monster.   60

57 *abatest thou*] do you slack

Augur. The monster is not come, and therefore I see Neptune is abused, whose rage will, I fear me, be both infinite and intolerable. Take in this virgin whose want of beauty hath saved her own life and [spoiled] all yours.

Ericthinis. We could not find any fairer.   65

Augur. Neptune will. Go, deliver her to her father.

Hebe. Fortunate Hebe, how shalt thou express thy joys? Nay, unhappy girl, that art not the fairest. Had it not been better for thee to have died with fame than to live with dishonour, to have preferred the safety of thy country and   70 rareness of thy beauty before sweetness of life and vanity of the world? But, alas, destiny would not have it so, destiny could not, for it asketh the beautifullest. I would, Hebe, thou hadst been beautifullest.

Ericthinis. Come, Hebe, here is no time for us to reason. It   75 had been best for us thou hadst been most beautiful.

Exeunt.

ACTUS QUINTUS   SCAENA TERTIA

[*Enter*] PHILLIDA, GALLATHEA.

Phillida. We met the virgin that should have been offered to Neptune. Belike either the custom is pardoned or she not thought fairest.

Gallathea. I cannot conjecture the cause, but I fear the event.

Phillida. Why should you fear? The god requireth no boy.   5

Gallathea. I would he did, then should I have no fear.

Phillida. I am glad he doth not, though, because if he did, I should have also cause to fear. But soft, what man or god is this? Let us closely withdraw ourselves into the thickets.

Exeunt ambo.

63 *want*] lack   64 [*spoiled*]] Omitted from Quarto

181

Enter NEPTUNE *alone.*

Neptune. And do men begin to be equal with gods, seeking 10
by craft to overreach them that by power oversee them? Do
they dote so much on their daughters that they stick not to
dally with our deities? Well shall the inhabitants see that
destiny cannot be prevented by craft, nor my anger be
appeased by submission. I will make havoc of Diana's 15
nymphs, my temple shall be dyed with maidens' blood,
and there shall be nothing more vile than to be a virgin. To
be young and fair shall be accounted shame and punishment, insomuch as it shall be thought as dishonourable to
be honest as fortunate to be deformed. 20

Enter DIANA *with her Nymphs.*

Diana. Oh, Neptune, hast thou forgotten thyself, or wilt
thou clean forsake me? Hath Diana therefore brought danger to her nymphs because they be chaste? Shall virtue suffer both pain and shame, which always deserveth praise
and honour? 25

Enter VENUS.

Venus. Praise and honour, Neptune? Nothing less, except it
be commendable to be coy and honourable to be peevish.
Sweet Neptune, if Venus can do anything, let her try it in
this one thing, that Diana may find as small comfort at thy
hands as love hath found courtesy at hers. 30

This is she that hateth sweet delights, envieth loving
desires, masketh wanton eyes, stoppeth amorous ears, bri-
dleth youthful mouths, and under a name, or a word, constancy, entertaineth all kind of cruelty. She hath taken my
son, Cupid, my lovely son, using him like a prentice, whip- 35
ping him like a slave, scorning him like a beast. Therefore,
Neptune, I entreat thee, by no other god than the god of
love, that thou evil entreat this goddess of hate.

Neptune. I muse not a little to see you two in this place, at
this time, and about this matter. But what say you, Diana? 40
Have you Cupid captive?

12 *stick not*] See II.ii.22n. 20 *honest*] chaste 28 *can do anything*] has influence
over you in any way 32 *masketh*] covers 38 *evil entreat*] treat harshly

182

Diana. I say there is nothing more vain than to dispute with
Venus, whose untamed affections have bred more brawls
in heaven than is fit to repeat in earth or possible to
recount in number. I have Cupid, and will keep him, not 45
to dandle in my lap, whom I abhor in my heart, but to
laugh him to scorn, that hath made in my virgins' hearts
such deep scars.
Venus. Scars, Diana, call you them that I know to be bleed-
ing wounds? Alas, weak deity, it stretcheth not so far both 50
to abate the sharpness of his arrows and to heal the hurts.
No, love's wounds when they seem green, rankle, and,
having a smooth skin without, fester to the death within.
Therefore, Neptune, if ever Venus stood thee in stead,
furthered thy fancies, or shall at all times be at thy com- 55
mand, let either Diana bring her virgins to a continual
massacre or release Cupid of his martyrdom.
Diana. It is known, Venus, that your tongue is as unruly as
your thoughts, and your thoughts as unstayed as your
eyes. Diana cannot chatter, Venus cannot choose. 60
Venus. It is an honour for Diana to have Venus mean ill
when she so speaketh well, but you shall see I come not to
trifle. Therefore once again, Neptune, if that be not buried
which can never die – fancy – or that quenched which
must ever burn – affection – show thyself the same 65
Neptune that I knew thee to be when thou wast a shepherd, and let not Venus' words be vain in thine ears, since
thine were imprinted in my heart.
Neptune. It were unfit that goddesses should strive, and it
were unreasonable that I should not yield, and therefore, 70
to please both, both attend. Diana I must honour, her
virtue deserveth no less; but Venus I must love, I must
confess so much. Diana, restore Cupid to Venus, and I will
forever release the sacrifice of virgins. If, therefore, you
love your nymphs as she doth her son, or prefer not a pri- 75
vate grudge before a common grief, answer what you will
do.

52 *green*] fresh   60 *choose*] help herself

183

Diana. I account not the choice hard, for had I twenty
Cupids I would deliver them all to save one virgin,
knowing love to be a thing of all the vainest, virginity to 80
be a virtue of all the noblest. I yield. Larissa, bring out
Cupid. [*Exit* LARISSA.] And now shall it be said that Cupid
saved those he thought to spoil.
Venus. I agree to this willingly, for I will be wary how my
son wander again. But Diana cannot forbid him to wound. 85
Diana. Yes, chastity is not within the level of his bow.
Venus. But beauty is a fair mark to hit.
Neptune. Well, I am glad you are agreed, and say that Nep-
tune hath dealt well with Beauty and Chastity.
                    Enter CUPID [*with* LARISSA].
Diana. Here, take your son.   90
Venus. Sir boy, where have you been? Always taken, first
by Sappho, now by Diana! How happeneth it, you un-
happy elf?
Cupid. Coming through Diana's woods, and seeing so
many fair faces with fond hearts, I thought, for my sport, 95
to make them smart; and so was taken by Diana.
Venus. I am glad I have you.
Diana. And I am glad I am rid of him.
Venus. Alas, poor boy, thy wings clipped? Thy brands
quenched? Thy bow burnt and thy arrows broke?   100
Cupid. Aye, but it skilleth not. I bear now mine arrows in
mine eyes, my wings on my thoughts, my brands in mine
ears, my bow in my mouth, so as I can wound with
looking, fly with thinking, burn with hearing, shoot with
speaking.   105
Venus. Well, you shall up to heaven with me, for on earth
thou wilt lose me.
            Enter TYTERUS, MELEBEUS [*from one direction*],
            GALLATHEA *and* PHILLIDA [*from another*].

87 *fair mark*] pun: both 'a legitimate target' and 'an agreeable object'   91-2 *first*
by Sappho] An allusion to Lyly's earlier play, *Sappho and Phao*, in which Cupid
renounces Venus and yields up his power to Sappho.   92-3 *unhappy*] unfortunate   101 *skilleth not*] does not matter

184

Neptune. But soft, what be these?

Tyterus. Those that have offended thee to save their
daughters. 110

Neptune. Why, had you a fair daughter?

Tyterus. Aye, and Melebeus a fair daughter.

Neptune. Where be they?

Melebeus. In yonder woods, and methinks I see them
coming. 115

Neptune. Well, your deserts have not gotten pardon, but
these goddesses' jars.

Melebeus. This is my daughter, my sweet Phillida.

Tyterus. And this is my fair Gallathea.

Gallathea. Unfortunate Gallathea, if this be Phillida! 120

Phillida. Accursed Phillida, if that be Gallathea!

Gallathea. And wast thou all this while enamoured of
Phillida, that sweet Phillida?

Phillida. And couldst thou dote upon the face of a maiden,
thyself being one, on the face of fair Gallathea? 125

Neptune. Do you both, being maidens, love one another?

Gallathea. I had thought the habit agreeable with the sex,
and so burned in the fire of mine own fancies.

Phillida. I had thought that in the attire of a boy there could
not have lodged the body of a virgin, and so was inflamed 130
with a sweet desire which now I find a sour deceit.

Diana. Now, things falling out as they do, you must leave
these fond, fond affections. Nature will have it so; necessity must.

Gallathea. I will never love any but Phillida; her love is 135
engraven in my heart with her eyes.

Phillida. Nor I any but Gallathea, whose faith is imprinted
in my thoughts by her words.

Neptune. An idle choice, strange and foolish, for one virgin
to dote on another, and to imagine a constant faith where 140
there can be no cause of affection. How like you this,
Venus?

108 *soft*] wait a moment   117 *jars*] disputes   127 *agreeable*] in accord with

185

Venus. I like well and allow it. They shall both be possessed
of their wishes, for never shall it be said that Nature or
Fortune shall overthrow Love and Faith. Is your loves 145
unspotted, begun with truth, continued with constancy,
and not to be altered till death?
Gallathea. Die, Gallathea, if thy love be not so!
Phillida. Accursed be thou, Phillida, if thy love be not so!
Diana. Suppose all this, Venus, what then? 150
Venus. Then shall it be seen that I can turn one of them to
be a man, and that I will.
Diana. Is it possible?
Venus. What is to love, or the mistress of love, unpossible?
Was it not Venus that did the like to Iphis and Ianthes? 155
How say ye? Are ye agreed, one to be a boy presently?
Phillida. I am content, so I may embrace Gallathea.
Gallathea. I wish it, so I may enjoy Phillida.
Melebeus. Soft, daughter, you must know whether I will
have you a son. 160
Tyterus. Take me with you, Gallathea, I will keep you as I
begat you, a daughter.
Melebeus. Tyterus, let yours be a boy, and if you will; mine
shall not.
Tyterus. Nay, mine shall not; for by that means my young 165
son shall lose his inheritance.
Melebeus. Why then, get him to be made a maiden, and
then there is nothing lost.
Tyterus. If there be such changing, I would Venus could
make my wife a man. 170
Melebeus. Why?
Tyterus. Because she loves always to play with men.
Venus. Well, you are both fond; therefore agree to this
changing, or suffer your daughters to endure hard chance.
Melebeus. How say you, Tyterus, shall we refer it to Venus? 175

---

155 *Iphis and Ianthes*] Iphis, having been brought up as a boy to avoid a sentence
of death, was betrothed to another maiden, Ianthe. The latter was changed into a
youth by Isis in order to permit their union. 156 *presently*] immediately
161 *Take me with you*] Bear me in mind

Tyterus. I am content, because she is a goddess.
Venus. Neptune, you will not dislike it?
Neptune. Not I.
Venus. Nor you, Diana?
Diana. Not I.   180
Venus. Cupid shall not.
Cupid. I will not.
Venus. Then let us depart. Neither of them shall know
whose lot it shall be till they come to the church door. One
shall be. Doth it suffice?   185
Phillida. And satisfy us both, doth it not, Gallathea?
Gallathea. Yes, Phillida.

Enter RAFE, ROBIN *and* DICK.

Rafe. Come, Robin, I am glad I have met with thee, for now
we will make our father laugh at these tales.
Diana. What are these that so malapertly thrust themselves 190
into our companies?
Robin. Forsooth, madam, we are fortune tellers.
Venus. Fortune-tellers? Tell me my fortune.
Rafe. We do not mean fortune-tellers, we mean fortune
tellers. We can tell what fortune we have had these twelve 195
months in the woods.
Diana. Let them alone, they be but peevish.
Venus. Yet they will be as good as minstrels at the marriage,
to make us all merry.
Dick. Aye, ladies, we bear a very good consort.   200
Venus. Can you sing?
Rafe. Basely.
Venus. And you?
Dick. Meanly.
Venus. And what can you do?   205
Robin. If they double it, I will treble it.

---

184 *church door*] Marriages were traditionally solemnized at the church
door. 190 *malapertly*] impudently 197 *peevish*] foolish, perverse 200 *consort*]
harmony 202-6 *basely . . . treble it*] punning confirmation and denial of the abili-
ty to sing in three part harmony (base, tenor and treble)

Venus. Then shall ye go with us, and sing Hymen before the marriage. Are you content?

Rafe. Content? Never better content, for there we shall be sure to fill our bellies with capons' rumps or some such 210 dainty dishes.

Venus. Then follow us.

Exeunt. [GALLATHEA *remains.*]

207 *sing Hymen*] perform a marriage song   208-9 *content / content*] satisfied / stuffing

The Epilogue

Gallathea. Go all, 'tis I only that conclude all. You ladies
may see that Venus can make constancy fickleness,
courage cowardice, modesty lightness, working things
impossible in your sex, and tempering hardest hearts like
softest wool. Yield, ladies, yield to love, ladies,   5
which lurketh under your eyelids whilst you sleep, and
playeth with your heartstrings whilst you wake, whose
sweetness never breedeth satiety, labour weariness, nor
grief bitterness. Cupid was begotten in a mist, nursed in
clouds, and sucking only upon conceits. Confess him a   10
conqueror, whom ye ought to regard, sith it is unpossible
to resist; for this is infallible, that love conquereth all
things but itself, and ladies all hearts but their own.

[*Exit.*]

Finis

11 *regard*] respect, venerate

Fyfield*Books*

Two millennia of essential classics
The extensive Fyfield*Books* list includes

Djuna Barnes *The Book of Repulsive Women and other poems*
edited by Rebecca Loncraine

Elizabeth Barrett Browning *Selected Poems* edited by Malcolm Hicks

Charles Baudelaire *Complete Poems in French and English*
translated by Walter Martin

The Brontë Sisters *Selected Poems* edited by Stevie Davies

Lewis Carroll *Selected Poems* edited by Keith Silver

Thomas Chatterton *Selected Poems* edited by Grevel Lindop

John Clare *By Himself* edited by Eric Robinson and David Powell

Samuel Taylor Coleridge *Selected Poetry* edited by William Empson and David Pirie

John Donne *Selected Letters* edited by P.M. Oliver

Oliver Goldsmith *Selected Writings* edited by John Lucas

Victor Hugo *Selected Poetry in French and English*
translated by Steven Monte

Wyndham Lewis *Collected Poems and Plays* edited by Alan Munton

Charles Lamb *Selected Writings* edited by J.E. Morpurgo

Ben Jonson *Epigrams and The Forest* edited by Richard Dutton

Giacomo Leopardi *The Canti with a selection of his prose*
translated by J.G. Nichols

Andrew Marvell *Selected Poems* edited by Bill Hutchings

Charlotte Mew *Collected Poems and Selected Prose*
edited by Val Warner

Michelangelo *Sonnets* translated by Elizabeth Jennings, introduction by Michael Ayrton

William Morris *Selected Poems* edited by Peter Faulkner

Ovid *Amores* translated by Tom Bishop

Edgar Allan Poe *Poems and Essays on Poetry* edited by C.H. Sisson

Restoration Bawdy edited by John Adlard

Rainer Maria Rilke *Sonnets to Orpheus and Letters to a Young Poet*
translated by Stephen Cohn

Christina Rossetti *Selected Poems* edited by C.H. Sisson

Sir Walter Scott *Selected Poems* edited by James Reed

Sir Philip Sidney *Selected Writings* edited by Richard Dutton

Henry Howard, Earl of Surrey *Selected Poems* edited by Dennis Keene

Algernon Charles Swinburne *Selected Poems* edited by L.M. Findlay

Oscar Wilde *Selected Poems* edited by Malcolm Hicks

Sir Thomas Wyatt *Selected Poems* edited by Hardiman Scott

For more information, including a full list of Fyfield*Books* and a contents list for each title, and details of how to order the books in the UK, visit the Fyfield website at www.fyfieldbooks.co.uk or email info@fyfieldbooks.co.uk. For information about Fyfield*Books* available in the United States and Canada, visit the Routledge website at www.routledge-ny.com.